Your Marketing Plan

*A Workbook For Effective
Business Promotion*

Chris Pryor

Oregon Small Business Development Center Network
99 W 10th Avenue, Suite 216
Eugene, OR 97401-3017

ISBN 1-878475-04-5

Preface

This workbook has been prepared for distribution by the Oregon Small Business Development Center Network. It is for those interested in starting their own business, as well as business owners with many years' experience who have never developed an organized marketing program.

"Marketing" is a term often misused and misunderstood in today's business world. This workbook is designed to give you the necessary tools to aid you in developing a marketing program to use in your business.

Marketing is not a simple task, but it is an extremely important one. You must be willing to give the time and effort required. You must be willing to look for, and accept, your own liabilities and shortcomings. You must be willing to make changes in the way you do business to accommodate marketing demands.

Promotion is the action element of marketing. Promotion includes EVERY instance of contact you have with your customers, and everything you say or do that might influence how you are perceived by them. And while advertising is, and always will be, an extremely important part of good marketing, it is only part of a much larger picture. The main objective of this workbook is to show how to use all the different promotional options you have available to you.

Chris Pryor is Marketing Supervisor for the Willamalane Park & Recreation District in Springfield, Oregon. His responsibilities include marketing research, strategic planning and promotional development and implementation. Pryor has experience working with both public and private organizations. He conducts seminars and workshops on marketing and advertising throughout the state and serves as president of the Southwest Oregon Chapter of the American Marketing Association.

Table of Contents

How to Use This Workbook

This workbook will become the "blueprint" for your business marketing. Each section covers a specific area of market planning and promotion and contains fill-in pages where you can insert information about your own organization.

Step 1: Read the workbook quickly to get a "feel" for its layout.

Step 2: Read the workbook more carefully but do not fill in the blanks.

Step 3: Begin to fill in some of the work sheets.

It isn't absolutely critical that you do this workbook in sequence. If you find a page you can do easily then fill it in. But, as you complete each section of the workbook, you may want to go back and change some of your assumptions, so . . .

WORK IN PENCIL

Step 4: Identify pages you can't complete right now.

No one can answer every question in this book without looking up information. Some questions will require "hard" information, like numbers and percentages; others will require "soft" information which is either your best guess, or an assumption based on some other factor. Don't use soft information if you have access to hard facts.

Step 5: Complete all the pages in this workbook.

Step 6: Use the information you have compiled in this workbook.

Refer to it as you perform your advertising tasks. Everything in this workbook is necessary and important to effective promotion.

The Need for Marketing

Why do People Have to Market Themselves?

Imagine throwing a party and not telling anyone about it? Running a business without marketing is virtually the same thing. You may have the most exciting products or the finest services available, but you must let people know they exist. Most small business owners don't understand the importance of advertising. Competition for customers is keen, and the world has grown too large for most businesses to rely upon "word-of-mouth" as their principal form of marketing.

Does Marketing Really Work?

If done right, yes. But good marketing requires a commitment from the entire organization. Any marketing program will fail if the wrong products are being offered at the wrong price or time. But if you use marketing to present the products customers want, at a price they are willing to pay, it can only spell success. YOU will have made it work - not your advertising.

But I Already Advertise!

Probably you do. But good marketing is more than just good advertising. Most small business owners don't fully understand their advertising. They don't create messages that work well with their customers or they fail to reach their customers with that message. This workbook can provide you with the tools to improve the advertising you're already doing.

Does it Have to be Expensive?

No. But it may cost more than you THINK it should. The most effective marketing is that which does the job without wasted time or money. By learning more about your customers, your products, and how to prepare messages which take advantage of that knowledge, you can make the best use of your advertising dollars.

Can I Hire Someone to do it for Me?

Yes. But this workbook is designed to enable you to do many of your marketing tasks yourself. You will prepare your own marketing plan, establish your own promotional outline and determine which media best suit your needs. You will be able to write your own advertising copy, or review copy written for you by someone else. Best of all, when you do reach that point when you need professional help, you will save time and money by having identified much of the information this person needs to develop a marketing program for you.

A Word about Artwork and Production.

The creation of effective advertising artwork and layouts, or quality radio and television production is not easy. The work that graphic artists, designers and producers perform requires years of experience. Poor advertising production is worse than no advertising at all because you may get no results and may even create a poor image for your company. Resist the temptation to try and do your own artwork.

Not all advertising situations require that you hire an advertising agency. In many instances a television station can help you produce TV ads or a radio station can help write your radio ads. This workbook will help you create the basic elements of good advertising which can then be quickly and effectively produced.

Marketing and its Mission

Because simple things are easier to remember, here is a simple definition of marketing.

Marketing is a process through which two people make an exchange that benefits both.

Every marketing program must have an ultimate purpose, a "Mission." The Mission Statement is probably one of the hardest things to do, yet it is one of the most important. These few words are the heart of why you are in business. They express both your vision and your philosophy of doing business. Everything else you do or say stems from this statement.

Step 1: Define your internal reasons for being in business.

A good Mission Statement is short and direct. It summarizes your most fundamental reasons for being in business, without going into long explanations or definitions. It must reflect the following points:

1. What makes us special or different?
2. What basic human needs do we satisfy?
3. What are the core values that drive our actions?

On the following page, identify your own reasons for being in *this* particular business. Don't just say "To make a lot of money." If that's your mission, you should be counterfeiting.

Step 2: Define the external influences on your business.

Business cannot occur within a vacuum. All business operations are constantly influenced by a combination of external conditions or environments. These environments include:

1. Social and cultural values
2. Economic conditions
3. Political and legal restrictions
4. Competitors
5. Advances in technology

Note the significant elements within each of these environments that affect the way you do business. Identify the one area which most influences the way you do business and give it a priority of 1. Give the second most influential factor a 2, and so on.

Step 3: Create a Mission Statement.

A good Mission Statement can adequately address all three of your reasons for being in business, and reflect the environment in which you operate. It must be brief, no more than 25 words. You should be able to quote your Mission Statement from memory because it influences every decision you make.

It should evoke emotion and stimulate attachment from people. Eliminate adjectives or qualifiers from the statement because they simply confuse the central idea. Deal with what the organization can be now rather than what it might be in the future. Future plans should be dealt with in the form of Goals.

Don't let the thought of focusing your business into one simple statement fool you. Major corporations spend many hours refining their mission down to a few simple words. A mission statement's importance is not based on its length. Mission statements work because they reach the absolute *heart* of what your company is doing. A Mission Statement you can't remember is a Mission Statement you won't use.

Marketing and its Mission

Step 1: Internal reasons for being in business.

      1. What makes us special or different?

_____

_____

      2. What basic human needs do we satisfy?

_____

_____

      3. What are the core values that drive our actions?

_____

_____

Step 2: External influences on my business.

      1. Significant social or cultural values   Priority_____

_____

_____

      2. Significant economic conditions   Priority_____

_____

_____

      3. Significant political or legal restrictions   Priority_____

_____

_____

      4. Significant competitive factors   Priority_____

_____

_____

      5. Significant advances in technology   Priority_____

_____

_____

Step 3: Your Mission Statement (25 words or less).

_____

_____

_____

_____

Marketing Research

Marketing research should be the starting point for any market planning or promotion. Smart advertisers use marketing research to locate and identify their customers, develop products to meet customer needs, and select the most effective ways to communicate information about the product to these buyers. The more you know about your customers, the more effective and economical your advertising will be.

There are four types of research you can use: **a.** information within your own files, **b.** information available to everyone in your industry (known as secondary sources), **c.** research you do yourself, and **d.** research you pay to have done.

Step 1: Locate existing sources of information.

Use the following checklist to help you locate information that already exists.

Your customer files - Most companies keep records about clients, employees and sales calls. Go through your files and compile information about where customers are located, the products they order, their usual buying practices, methods of payment, and any other information that might help you better understand them.

U.S. Census - The U.S. Census has information concerning both the buying public and your industry. You can purchase Census information inexpensively from the government, or use the Census information available at your library.

Associations - Most industries have a national association, which can be one of your most valuable sources of information. Call or write them. They will be happy to send you what they have or refer you to others who have market information.

Data Bases - With a computer and a modem you have access to data bases located all over North America. Compuserve, GEnie, Dialog, and Western Union's Infomaster are just a few.

Libraries - The reference section of most large libraries provides a wealth of information. The reference librarian knows what they have and what might be useful to you.

The Small Business Administration - The SBA publishes dozens of pamphlets and workbooks on most business subjects. The address of the SBA in Washington, DC is included with the list of resources at the end of this workbook.

You will find a list of other resources at the end of this workbook which will aid you in formulating your promotions. You may already know the trade publications available in your industry. If you don't, go to the public library, or your community college, and consult the reference librarian.

Step 2: Conduct a customer profile survey.

Print these questions on a half sheet of stiff paper. Pick one week each quarter and distribute the form to everyone who visits your business. Give each person a pencil and encourage him to fill out the form before departing. Assure everyone you are only seeking general information. Avoid the temptation to include a place for the individual's name and address. People will think you are just compiling a mailing list, and the resulting information will be extremely biased. Ask respondents to be sure and drop the completed form in a box by the entrance. At the end of the week collect the completed forms and tabulate the results.

Step 3: Perform a random quarterly customer satisfaction review.

Make about 200 copies of the survey form. For one week each quarter, distribute the forms to randomly selected customers. Ask them to complete the form and place it in a provided box. By actively passing out the surveys, you will greatly increase your chance of having them filled-out. Tabulate the forms on a large sheet of paper, using hashmarks for each response.

Marketing Research

Step 1: Checklist of secondary sources.

	Maintained Internally	Have Access to	Need to Locate Source
1. Your Customer files	( )	( )	( )
2. U.S. Census	( )	( )	( )
3. Associations	( )	( )	( )
4. Data Bases	( )	( )	( )
5. Libraries	( )	( )	( )
6. The SBA	( )	( )	( )

Step 2: Sample customer profile survey.

CUSTOMER PROFILE SURVEY

Will you take a moment to help us? We are conducting a brief audit survey as part of an effort to better serve our customers. Please fill out this survey form and drop it in the box provided. Do not give your name or address. This survey is for statistical information only. No one will call you, or mail you anything. Thank you for your help.

1. Which radio station do you listen to *most* often?

2. Which section of the newspaper do you read *most* often?

3. What is your residential zip code? _____

4. Have you visited this business before?   ( ) Yes   ( ) No

5. Are you: ( ) Male   ( ) Female

6. Which of these general ranges includes your age?
   ( ) 18-24   ( ) 25-34   ( ) 35-49   ( ) 50-54   ( ) 55 or older

7. What is your occupation? Not where you work, but the kind of work you do.
   _____

8. Which of the following broad ranges includes your annual household income?
   ( ) Below $10,000   ( ) $10,000-$30,000   ( ) $30,000-$60,000   ( ) Over $60,000

THANK YOU VERY MUCH FOR YOUR ASSISTANCE!

Marketing Research

Step 3: Quarterly random customer satisfaction review.

CUSTOMER SATISFACTION SURVEY

In our continuing effort to improve the quality of service we provide, we seek the honest opinions of customers like yourself. Please take a minute to answer the questions below and put the completed form in the box near the front. Thank you for your help.

1. Please rate your experience today in each of the following categories:

	Excellent	Good	Average	Fair	Poor
A. Quality of the products	( )	( )	( )	( )	( )
B. Value for the money	( )	( )	( )	( )	( )
C. Ease of getting to and from this store	( )	( )	( )	( )	( )
D. Friendliness and courtesy of the employees	( )	( )	( )	( )	( )
E. Efficiency of the service	( )	( )	( )	( )	( )
F. Cleanliness and appearance of the store	( )	( )	( )	( )	( )

2. What is the one thing you like most about this store?

_____

3. What things do you like least, or would like to see changed?

_____

4. Are there any additional products or services you would like to see us offer?

_____

Please answer the following general questions about yourself.

5. How did you arrive at the store today?

    ( ) Car   ( ) Walked   ( ) Bus   ( ) Bike   ( ) Other _____

6. Which radio station do you listen to *most* often? _____

7. Do you read the newspaper on a regular basis (at least three out of every four issues)?

    ( ) Yes   ( ) No   ( ) Don't know

8. Please indicate if you are: ( ) Male   ( ) Female

9. Which of the following ranges includes your age?

    ( ) 18-24   ( ) 25-34   ( ) 35-49   ( ) 50-54   ( ) 55 or older

THANK YOU VERY MUCH FOR YOUR ASSISTANCE!

Marketing Research

Step 4: Research organization evaluation form.

Sometimes the complexity of the information you need requires you to use an outside research firm to do the work. Subjective questions dealing with why people feel the way they do or their opinions on a subject, require careful wording and execution to ensure accurate answers. To be effective, a third (impartial) party such as a professional marketing research organization, is required to gain this information.

Use this work sheet to assist in evaluating outside marketing research organizations.

Name _____

Address _____

Phone _____   Contact _____

EVALUATION CRITERIA   COMMENTS

( ) List of current clients   _____

( ) Samples of work done   _____

( ) References from clients   _____

( ) Facilities and staff   _____

( ) Company materials   _____

EVALUATION OF THE FIRM'S CAPABILITIES

Has this agency done research for similar organizations?	( ) Yes	( ) Somewhat	( ) No
Are the people at the firm easy to work with?	( ) Yes	( ) Somewhat	( ) No
Does this firm have experience in questionnaire design?	( ) Yes	( ) Somewhat	( ) No
Is the firm fully capable in all forms of implementation?	( ) Yes	( ) Somewhat	( ) No
Does the firm have adequate computer tabulating capability?	( ) Yes	( ) Somewhat	( ) No
Are the firm's reports clear and easy to understand	( ) Yes	( ) Somewhat	( ) No
Are the data analysts qualified and experienced?	( ) Yes	( ) Somewhat	( ) No
Do the company's references give good ratings?	( ) Yes	( ) Somewhat	( ) No

11

Who - Defining Your Customers

If you expect to be successful you must know as much as you can about your customers.

Your customers are the most important part of your business. Without customers you wouldn't be in business. It's critical to carefully analyze who your customers are, how much and how often they buy from you, and why they do business with you rather than someone else.

Demographics

Demographics are the identifiable characteristics of people, such as age, sex, occupation, income, etc. They are important because they represent the natural categories of customers.

Some of the more common demographic identifiers include:

Sex - Each sex exhibits very different habits when it comes to purchasing. Knowing if your market is predominantly male or female is fundamental to any market planning.

Age - is second only to sex as the most important demographic to measure your market. Different age groups have significantly different habits and interests.

Income - is a good indicator because it often shows whether or not the customer has the ability in addition to the desire to buy.

Occupation - relates closely to age, income, and education. May in itself represent a purchase motivation.

Location - can be designated in any of several different ways, such as zip code, address, city, state, shopping area, neighborhood, etc. Many businesses discover that the majority of their business comes from specific locations rather than from all over town.

The customers of any given business can usually be distributed among these standard demographic groups. The following work sheet will help you determine what percent of your customers fall within each group's divisions.

Use the results of your Customer Profile Survey to complete the following work sheet.

Step 1: Tabulating the Customer Profile Survey on Page 9.

Use a separate sheet of graph paper for each question on the survey. Write the possible responses to the question down the left side of the page. Now go through the questionnaires one by one and mark off the actual answers given by respondents. The sex question, for example would look like this:

Men   ✝✝✝ ✝✝✝ ✝✝✝ ✝✝✝ ✝✝✝ |||

Women   ✝✝✝ ✝✝✝ ✝✝✝ ✝✝✝ ✝✝✝ ✝✝✝ ✝✝✝ |

When you have entered all the questionnaires, take the total for each response and divide it by the total number of questionnaires collected. If you have 400 questionnaires and 123 men, divide 123 by 400 to arrive at .3075, or 30.75% (just move the decimal point two places to the right to get a percent). You now know that approximately 30.75% of your customers are men.

Who - Defining Your Customers

Step 1: Use the completed and tabulated Customer Profile Survey on Page 9.

Step 2: List your customers by **Sex.**

_____% Male   _____% Female

Step 3: List your customers by **Age.**

_____% 18-24   _____% 25-34

_____% 35-49   _____% 50-55

_____% Over 55

Step 4: List your customers by **Income.**

_____% Under $10,000   _____% $10,000-$30,000

_____% $30,000-$60,000   _____% Over $60,000

Step 5: List your customers by **Occupation.**

_____% Admin.   _____% Profes.   _____% Semi-Profes.

_____% Clerical   _____% Blue Collar   _____% Student

_____% Homemaker   _____% Retired   _____% Disabled/Unemp.

Step 6: List your customers by **Location.**

_____% Zip #(   )   _____% Zip #(   )   _____% Zip #(   )

_____% Zip #(   )   _____% Zip #(   )   _____% Zip #(   )

Segmenting Markets

It comes as no surprise that different people have different tastes and attitudes. What is important to the marketer is the fact that different demographic *groups* have widely different buying habits and product preferences.

The 80/20 rule of marketing notes that 80% of a typical company's business is probably done with 20% of its customers. Blanket statements such as this generally don't hold up in every case, but the basic concept applies. Some people just naturally buy more of your product, or buy more often, than others. And experience has shown that these natural divisions most often occur along standard demographic lines. The process of splitting out the various interest groups from the rest of the people who buy your products is called Market Segmentation.

Step 1: Organize your market groupings.

Review the demographic breakdowns on the previous page. Within each demographic, locate the category that has the *largest* percentage of customers and insert that category's description in Market 1. Continue with the next largest sub-group in Market 2 and so on until you have listed all the percentages. Markets 1 and 2 should have a description in every space.

Market 1.

Sex _____   Age _____   Income _____

Occup. _____   Location _____

Market 2.

Sex _____   Age _____   Income _____

Occup. _____   Location _____

Market 3.

Sex _____   Age _____   Income _____

Occup. _____   Location _____

Market 4.

Sex _____   Age _____   Income _____

Occup. _____   Location _____

Market 5.

Sex _____   Age _____   Income _____

Occup. _____   Location _____

Targeting Markets

Very few businesses have the money or the time to market to every segment of the public. Some market segments buy so little it isn't worth the effort. Others require a more than average share of attention to keep them buying. If you know who the critical 20% of your customers are, it stands to reason they are the group you most want to reinforce with your advertising. This process is called "targeting" your market because you want to focus in on a specific central group of consumers.

Step 1: Copy this work sheet.

Complete the work sheet below for each product or service, or class of products or services you sell, and for each market group defined on the previous page.

Step 2: List the physical characteristics of your target market.

Copy these from the previous page and insert in the appropriate places on the work sheet. If the market group being listed is Group 1 or Group 2, indicate it as a Target Market. All other groups should be classed as Secondary.

TARGET MARKET GROUP

1. Sex   Male _____% 　　　Female _____%

2. Age range   From _____ 　　　To _____

3. Income range From $_____ 　　　To $_____

4. Occupation   _____ or _____

6. Location   _____

Step 3: Note the motivational characteristics of your target market.

For many years, marketers have defined their markets by physical characteristics alone. They are now beginning to look at consumer needs and product benefits to see how they relate to buying. We now know that different demographic groups maintain fairly consistent needs and are motivated by similar benefits. Characterizing a market's needs and benefits is just as important as cataloguing its physical attributes.

For example, all people need toothpaste. However, the *need* of the young single buyer is attractiveness, while the *need* of the parent is to preserve the health of a child. Thus the benefit of toothpaste to the younger buyer is improved appearance while the parent recognizes the benefit of reduced cavities.

7. What specific benefit do you believe this group seeks by using the product or service?

_____

_____

8. What personal needs do you believe will be satisfied by using the product or service?

_____

_____

What - Defining Your Products

Products include services and fall into two basic categories - Industrial and Consumer.

Industrial Products - are those things which are used to create other goods, or in servicing the production of goods and services.

Consumer Products - are those things which can be purchased by the intended end user.

For the purpose of this workbook we will often refer to both products and services as "products."

Step 1: Copy this work sheet for each product you sell.

You may also combine your products into *families* which have similar target markets, product characteristics, benefits and for which you plan to use similar marketing methods.

Step 2: Describe the physical characteristics of the product.

Most people select products based on what it looks like or how it's packaged. Attractive physical appearance is crucial because in most instances you can't be there to motivate the customer or give additional information. The product must sell itself. And people, unfortunately, don't tend to give as much weight to functionality as they do beauty. As a result, pretty products get chosen over their uglier, but more useful, cousins. It's not logical, but marketing to people doesn't always make sense.

Look at your own product from a purely visual standpoint. Ignore for the moment what it does. In the section to the right note those elements of the product package that are attractive as strengths and those that are ugly or ungainly as weaknesses. Regardless of which is which, you should consider reinforcing the attractive elements and eliminating the ugly ones. You don't need the most expensive package in the world, but you should never scrimp on the first impression. As the slogan says "You don't get a second chance to make a first impression."

Step 3: Describe the physical benefits of the product.

If your packaging and product appearance attracted attention, the customer will stop and consider how the product can physically benefit his or her life. For a piece of clothing, they must believe its beauty will make them more beautiful. People only buy products if their stated purpose satisfies their personal needs. In marketing terms that translates to "People don't need drills . . . they need ways to make holes."

Consider the basic physical need your product satisfies. What does your customer need to accomplish by the use of your product? List those needs which only your product can satisfy as primary. Needs which your product, as well as others, can satisfy are secondary. Use your imagination to put yourself in the customer's place. Focus on their real need to have it, not your real need to sell it.

Step 4: Describe the psychological needs the product will satisfy.

People also buy products because they satisfy psychological needs. In many ways these psychological needs act more strongly on the buying decision than the physical benefits. Luxury items are excellent examples of the things we buy because thay satisfy pshchological needs. After all who really *needs* a five karat diamond ring or a BMW. Marketers don't judge a buyer's real needs, they satisfy perceived needs. Who is to say one need is more legitimate than another.

List the psychological needs your product satisfies. A few needs may be conscious, but more often than not, even the buyer doesn't understand all the reasons they want a product. Some examples of psychological needs might include such words as prestige, vanity, security, fear, pleasure, gratification, altruism, the need to belong, pride, loyalty, memory, hope, or love. Watch a Kodak commercial closely. They're not selling film. They're selling memories.

What - Defining Your Products

Step 2: Describe the physical characteristics of the product.

Strengths	Weaknesses
_____	_____
_____	_____
_____	_____
_____	_____
_____	_____
_____	_____
_____	_____

Step 3: Describe the physical benefits of the product.

Primary	Secondary
_____	_____
_____	_____
_____	_____
_____	_____
_____	_____
_____	_____
_____	_____

Step 4: Describe the psychological needs the product will satisfy.

Conscious	Unconscious
_____	_____
_____	_____
_____	_____
_____	_____
_____	_____
_____	_____

The Product Profile

Consumers consciously evaluate retail products by the variable factors of price and quality. Of course there are a host of other conscious and unconscious factors which can govern behavior, but price and quality are the two factors common to nearly all purchase decisions.

Each product has a customer identity, or profile, based on the balance of these two variables. Competition *begins* by evaluating the perceived differences in each product's basic profile. Product profiles tend to run in cycles based on product age. Examples of the four basic profile combinations are:

> *Low Price/High Quality* – An ideal product profile which balances price and quality in the consumer's favor. Most new businesses establish themselves with this profile because it competes so easily with the other three.

> *High Price/High Quality* – As demand for a product increases, producer's realize they can increase price assuming quality also remains high. Customers may accept the higher price due to unconscious factors such as prestige. Mercedes Benz, Curtis Mathes Television, Rolex, and Nikon are all representative of this group.

> *High Price/Low Quality* – Company's with older well-established products often fail to update them regularly. The potential for profit inherent in coasting on a quality reputation can be fatal once the public realizes the product no longer justifies the price. Customers, once betrayed, seldom give these products a second chance.

> *Low Price/Low Quality* – The "discount" philosophy of many mass merchandisers was once thought to be the wave of the future. Because product quality from discounter to discounter is the same, price assumes greater significance. Even small retailers offering a significantly better product for the same price (and letting the public know about it through adequate advertising) can effectively compete against the low price/low quality profile.

Step 1: Define your products' profiles.

Evaluate the price and quality of your major products and the perceived price/quality of your business as a whole. Mark the position of each product on the circle with an *x*. Now place a *y* on the circle in the position where you company fits as a whole.

Step 2: Identify your competitors' product profiles.

Identify your four major competitors and write their names in the indicated spaces. Note each one's overall profile on the cycle with a 1, 2, 3, or 4.

You may may want to skip this part until you have completed the section on competition in order to evaluate your competitors' overall business profiles. You can then return and complete this step.

The Product Profile

Step 1: Define your products' profiles.

Defining Your Product's Profile

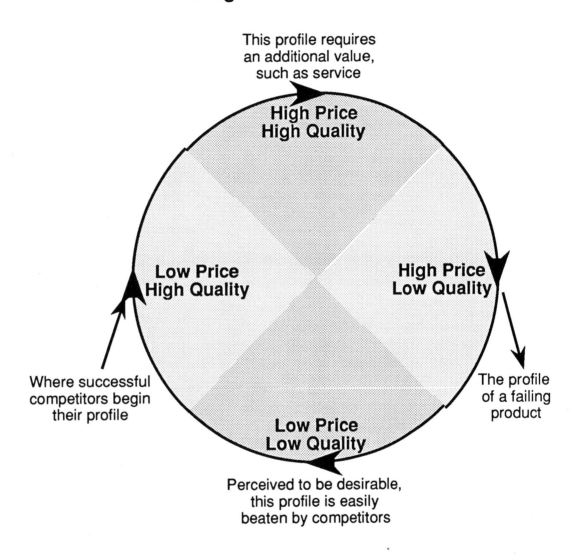

This profile requires an additional value, such as service

High Price High Quality

Low Price High Quality

High Price Low Quality

Low Price Low Quality

Where successful competitors begin their profile

The profile of a failing product

Perceived to be desirable, this profile is easily beaten by competitors

Step 2: Identify your competitors' product profiles.

Competitor #1 _____ Profile _____

Competitor #2 _____ Profile _____

Competitor #3 _____ Profile _____

Competitor #4 _____ Profile _____

When -
Product Life Cycles and Seasons

Every product has a lifespan, and your promotional priorities are also influenced by that product's place in its life cycle. For example, promoting for an established product is generally different from that of a new one. Pricing considerations for a declining product are considerably different than those for a growing one. Competition among new products is often keener than among established ones.

Step 1: Copy the following work sheet for each product you sell.

Step 2: Assign each product a place in the product life cycle.

Some of the factors influencing a product's position in the product life cycle include length of existence, visibility, familiarity, frequency of use, and popularity over alternative products.

Specific points in the life cycle

1. New Product - Just introduced, has little visibility.
2. Growing Purchase - People discover the product.
3. Established Position - Recognized in marketplace.
4. Maturity - Purchase is regular and habitual.
5. Loss of Value - Product begins to lose sales.
6. Declining Purchase - Significant decline in sales.

Current examples

Biologically engineered organisms
Personal computers
Unleaded gasoline
Campbell's Soup
Cigarettes
Anything "Disco"

Step 3: Understanding your product's "season."

Go to your ledger and get the gross sales figure for the previous year. Divide that figure by 12 to arrive at a monthly average. Your monthly average is the same as the Avg. line of this chart. Now examine the actual sales you made in each month of the last year. Place a dot in the appropriate monthly column to show how much your actual monthly sales differed from the average. If your average sales figure comes to $500 but your actual sales were $650, you did 30% better than the average for that month. You would therefore put your dot a little above the +25% line on the chart. Calculate the percent difference for each month until every column is marked. Now connect the dots to see your product's buying season.

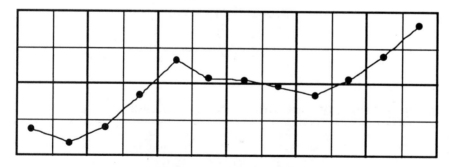

How to Calculate Percent Differences

Always divide the larger sales figure by the smaller one, then convert the resulting decimal to a percent. The percent is + if you divide actual sales by average sales and – if you must divide average sales by actual sales. Remember to throw away the 1 *first*, then move the decimal point two places to the right.

Example where *actual* is larger $650 ÷ $500 = 1.30 (throw away the 1 and move the decimal two
                                            places to the right) = +30%

Example where *average* is larger $500 ÷ $350 = 1.43 (throw away the 1 and move the decimal two
                                            places to the right) = –43%

When -
Product Life Cycles and Seasons

Step 1: Product identity.

PRODUCT _____

Step 2: Position on the product life cycle.

1( ) New Product   4( ) Maturity

2( ) Growing Purchase   5( ) Loss of Value

3( ) Established Position   6( ) Declining Purchase

Step 3: Chart your product's seasonality.

Product Buying Cycle

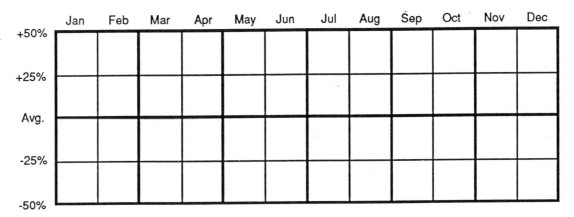

Where - Location and Distribution

To many business owners, the choice of a business location is simply a matter of being close to the customer. If you deal strictly in services, this may be right for you. However, manufacturers and retailers must receive products, or the raw materials to make products from outside suppliers who might be hundreds or even thousands of miles away. Your position as one link in a much longer distribution "chain" requires that you manage the supply end as well as the sale end.

In the simplest distribution chain, a manufacturer sells his product directly to a customer, just as in a farmer's roadside fruit stand. Complicated distribution chains such as those in the automobile industry may have a car maker dealing with a central distributor for small components from several different suppliers, and then using sales agents to sell finished cars to a wholesaler, who in turn resells the cars to individual dealerships, who in turn sell the cars to consumers. Of course to cover costs, each link in the chain must charge a higher price as they pass the cars on, causing the price to go up fast.

The advantage of these long chains usually centers on transportation, convenience, and availability. Distributors and wholesalers specialize in moving and storing large quantities of goods. Retailers also like the idea of calling one wholesaler to order their products rather than making many separate phone calls, and negotiating separate financial arrangements, with different suppliers. Manufacturers like distributors because they purchase large quantities of goods all at once and eliminate the need for further promotion. The lower price the wholesaler pays to the manufacturer is more than offset by the savings in marketing and transportation costs.

Step 1: Plot a distribution chain for each product you sell.

Copy this work sheet for each product which requires a unique distribution system. Use the Manufacturer Chain if you make products which someone else sells to the public, and the Retailer Chain of you sell directly to the end user. In the boxes note the number of suppliers, agents, distributors, retailers, and customers you deal with to sell your product. If you don't use a particular link draw a line through the box. On the lines below each box write the distance to the furthest major member of each group you work with.

Step 2: Evaluate the strengths of your distribution system.

In the spaces provided write down what works well within your distribution chain. It may be the ability to distribute products broadly through the use of wholesalers, the cost saving from selling to only one distributor, or the shortness of the chain itself. It may be the fact that it's a short chain. These advantages are what make your distribution cost effective.

Step 3: Assess the weaknesses of your system.

Do the same thing for your distribution chain's weaknesses. This might involve a major supplier being too far away, making transportation costs unreasonably high. Or, you may have too many links in the chain taking too large a cut of the profit. Sometimes selling outright to a wholesaler means you have no control over how the finished product is displayed or sold. By addressing weaknesses in your distribution chain you can often reduce distribution costs.

Where - Location and Distribution

Step 1: Plot your distribution chain.

Manufacturers Distribution Chain

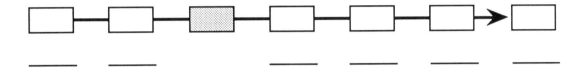

Retailers Distribution Chain

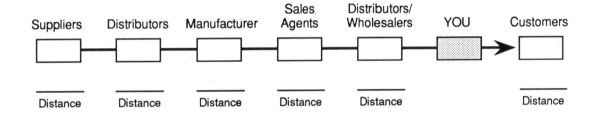

Step 2: Evaluate the strengths of your distribution system.

_____
_____
_____
_____

Step 3: Assess the weaknesses of your system.

_____
_____
_____
_____

Why - Satisfying Customer Needs

The marketing exchange requires you, as the seller, to provide a product with *values* which satisfy the *needs* of the buyer. This concept of values satisfying needs is fundamental to good marketing. But without a clear definition of the *consumer's* needs you cannot hope to provide an appropriate or appealing value. You should also remember that few needs are based solely on the product.

Step 1: Copy and complete the following page for each product you sell.

Step 2: Answer the questions concerning your product.

This will indicate the general needs the product satisfies.

Step 3: List four items a customer could buy to satisfy the same need.

These are competitive products. Example - if you sell toys, competitive products might include (in addition to other toys) such things as home computers, movie tickets or books. Since the need a toy satisfies is *entertainment*, these other products provide strong competition at the need level.

Step 4: Indicate why your product is unique or special.

These will become product values, or reasons why your product is not like the alternatives. These points should be addressed in your advertising.

Step 5: List your product's advantages.

Indicate what you believe to be the reasons why your product is a better choice to satisfy the need, as opposed to the four competitors listed in Step 3.

Step 6: List your product's disadvantages.

What qualities do the competitive products possess that make them superior or at least more salable than yours.

Why - Satisfying Customer Needs

Step 2: What general customer need does your product satisfy? Does it . . .

	Yes	Maybe	No
1. Make the buyer feel more important?	( )	( )	( )
2. Make the buyer happier?	( )	( )	( )
3. Make the buyer more comfortable?	( )	( )	( )
4. Make the buyer more prosperous?	( )	( )	( )
5. Work easier for the buyer?	( )	( )	( )
6. Provide greater security?	( )	( )	( )
7. Make the buyer more attractive?	( )	( )	( )
8. Make the buyer better liked?	( )	( )	( )
9. Will it give the buyer some distinction?	( )	( )	( )
10. Improve or protect the buyer's health?	( )	( )	( )
11. Appeal to the buyer as a bargain?	( )	( )	( )
12. Other _____			

Step 3: Alternative products (product competitors).

    A. _____

    B. _____

    C. _____

    D. _____

Step 4: Unique/special features of your product.

    A. _____

    B. _____

    C. _____

    D. _____

Step 5: Advantages of your product (over competition).

    A. _____

    B. _____

    C. _____

    D. _____

Step 6: Disadvantages of your product (as compared to competition).

    A. _____

    B. _____

    C. _____

    D. _____

Competitors

Many business owners assume that if there is no other store in town that offers the same products or services, they have no competition. By the same token, these same business owners may also write-off known competitors simply because they don't know anything about them. Both these assumptions are *usually* incorrect and *often* fatal.

Step 1: Insert the names and addresses of four major competitors.

    A. Name _____

         Address _____

    B. Name _____

         Address _____

    C. Name _____

         Address _____

    D. Name _____

         Address _____

Don't underestimate the potential impact of your competitors simply because you don't know anything about them. The best way to win any marketing campaign is to know the competition's position, their strengths and weaknesses.

Step 2: Perform a competitor analysis.

Gather the following information for each competitor you identified above. Don't provide opinions, just *observations*. This requires an actual visit to each competitor's business to see first hand what they're doing. If you are too well-known, or this is a problem, have someone whose opinion and judgement you trust do it for you. But above all be honest in your assessments.

Step 3: Assess your competitor's promotional efforts.

Actively seek out examples of each competitor's promotional materials. This includes newspaper ads, radio and TV spots, brochures and catalogues, etc.

1. **Are they eye-catching?** You can't sell anything unless you get the customer's attention.

2. **Do they make their point?** The message must be simple, clear and persuasive.

3. **Are they consistent in their approach?** Related materials reinforce and build on each other. Pieces that don't match, don't appear related.

4. **Do they offer legitimate value?** Customers will not buy without it.

Competitors

Step 2: Competitor analysis.

COMPETITOR _____

1. Products _____
2. Price _____
3. Quality _____
4. Product selection _____
5. Customer service _____
6. Product service _____
7. Reliability _____
8. Expertise _____
9. Image/Reputation _____
10. Location _____
11. Layout _____
12. Appearance _____
13. Sales methods _____
14. Credit policy _____
15. Availability _____
16. Management _____
17. Longevity/Stability _____

Step 3: Competitor promotional assessment.

Promotional Materials

Do they attract attention? _____

_____

Do they make their point? _____

_____

Are they consistent? _____

_____

What is the principle value offered? _____

_____

Competitive Position

Now that you have specific information about each of your competitors, evaluate each one's relative strengths and weaknesses as it relates to your own business.

Step 1: Rate your competitive position.

The following work sheet provides an item by item assessment of both you and your competitors.

For each area of comparison below, rank your business and each of the four competitors on a scale of 1 to 5, with 1 being lowest and 5 highest. Rate the one who performs best a 5, the one who performs second best a 4, third best a 3, etc.

1. **Products** - Which products do the better job?
2. **Price** - Consistency is generally the best plan.
3. **Quality** - How long does it last, how good are the materials and workmanship?
4. **Product selection** - How complete is the product line, what options are available?
5. **Customer service** - How politely and thoroughly is service performed?
6. **Product service** - Is the product serviced correctly and quickly?
7. **Reliability** - Does the product require frequent service or repair?
8. **Expertise** - The more knowledgeable the staff, the better.
9. **Image/Reputation** - How important or useful is the company or product name?
10. **Location** - Consider accessibility, parking, convenience and visibility.
11. **Layout** - Is the space efficiently utilized?
12. **Appearance** - Does the appearance match the customer's expectations?
13. **Sales methods** - Is the staff polite and effective at making sales?
14. **Credit policy** - Can customers use a variety of payment methods?
15. **Availability** - Does the customer have to wait for a product to arrive?
16. **Management** - Does the store owner take an active part in the business?
17. **Longevity/Stability** - In general, older businesses are considered more stable.
18. **Advertising** - Those who advertise are more visible than those who don't.

Step 2: Calculate your competitive ranking.

Total each column. The column with the HIGHEST number represents the business in the best competitive position and receives a rank of 1. The column with the LOWEST number represents the least competitive position and receives a rank of 5.

Add all the column totals together and divide by 5 to get the *average* competitive ranking. Divide each of the column totals by the sum of all the columns to get a *percent* of competitive market share (don't forget that percentages in calculations are always expressed as decimals; .53 = 53%).

$$\frac{\text{Column Total}}{\substack{\text{Sum of all Column} \\ \text{Totals}}} = \text{Percent (in decimal form)}$$

Competitive Position

Step 1: Rate your competitive position.

Factors	You	Competitor A	B	C	D
1. Products	_____	_____	_____	_____	_____
2. Price	_____	_____	_____	_____	_____
3. Quality	_____	_____	_____	_____	_____
4. Product selection	_____	_____	_____	_____	_____
5. Customer service	_____	_____	_____	_____	_____
6. Product service	_____	_____	_____	_____	_____
7. Reliability	_____	_____	_____	_____	_____
8. Expertise	_____	_____	_____	_____	_____
9. Image/Reputation	_____	_____	_____	_____	_____
10. Location	_____	_____	_____	_____	_____
11. Layout	_____	_____	_____	_____	_____
12. Appearance	_____	_____	_____	_____	_____
13. Sales methods	_____	_____	_____	_____	_____
14. Credit policy	_____	_____	_____	_____	_____
15. Availability	_____	_____	_____	_____	_____
16. Management	_____	_____	_____	_____	_____
17. Longevity/Stability	_____	_____	_____	_____	_____
18. Advertising	_____	_____	_____	_____	_____

Step 2: Calculate competitive rankings.

	You	A	B	C	D
Totals	_____	_____	_____	_____	_____
Rankings	_____	_____	_____	_____	_____
Average ranking	_____				
% competitive market share	_____%	_____%	_____%	_____%	_____%

Competitive Position

In addition to your competitive advantage over other businesses, you must also evaluate your competitive position in general. It's good to compare yourself to others, but you must also evaluate your business on an absolute scale.

Just because you may have a better location than any of your competitors, doesn't mean you have "the best" location. You must gain competitive advantage in ways that directly affect your dealings with the public.

Step 1: Identify who is strongest in each competitive area.

The list of factors includes many normally associated with sound competitive businesses. If you are truthfully the best provider of that factor, write in your own name. If not, indicate which of your competitors is best.

Step 2: Identify the four major advantages you have over your competitors.

These are areas where you rank at least 2 points higher than any of the other competitors.

Step 3: List the four areas of weakness as compared to your competition.

These are areas where your competition routinely ranks 3 or more.

Step 4: Indicate those areas where there is no competition.

Sometimes a particular product or feature is not available, even though a demand may exist. It might be a special product, a unique location, a new service, or a different image. These areas will become very important when you begin the process of market positioning.

Competitive Position

Step 1: Identify company image

Best traffic area	_____	Best access by car	_____
Most parking	_____	Free parking	_____
Easiest to find	_____	Best signs	_____
Best lit	_____	Best decorated	_____
Best staff attitude	_____	Best brochures	_____
Knowledgeable	_____	Best advertising	_____

Step 2: Areas of advantage over competition.

1. _____

2. _____

3. _____

4. _____

Step 3: Areas of weakness as compared to your competition.

1. _____

2. _____

3. _____

4. _____

Step 4: Areas of no competitive activity.

1. _____

2. _____

3. _____

4. _____

Your Image

"Image" is another marketing term many people use without really understanding the concept.

Image is nothing more than what other people believe about you. Just as an attractive product may be selected over an ugly one, an "attractive" company may be chosen over an "ugly" one. When buyers can't judge the value of the product, they judge the value of the seller.

Since the image you have with your customers is based on what they BELIEVE, rather than what is TRUE, it's important that what they believe is positive. It's up to you to insure this happens.

Step 1: Identify your company image with your customers.

Answer each of the questions below HONESTLY, and from the perspective of the customer. Since all the statements above are basically positive, a NO, or even a SOMETIMES, answer represents a potential image problem area.

	Yes	Sometimes	No
My business is seen as an attractive asset to the community.	( )	( )	( )
People feel it is prestigious to do business with me.	( )	( )	( )
My business gives a good value for the money spent.	( )	( )	( )
My product/service is felt to be among the best available.	( )	( )	( )
My staff is considered friendly and knowledgeable.	( )	( )	( )
People would rather do business with me.	( )	( )	( )
Most people instantly recognize my company's name.	( )	( )	( )
It is easier to use my product/service than do-it-yourself.	( )	( )	( )
I haven't heard any negative comments in a long time.	( )	( )	( )
My business is well-known in the community.	( )	( )	( )
My business is considered expert in my field.	( )	( )	( )
My products or services deliver real results.	( )	( )	( )
People don't have any problem getting to my business.	( )	( )	( )

Step 2: How are opinions about you formed?

Each of the methods listed below is a common method of creating and spreading opinions and perceptions regarding your business. Consider each one and indicate next to it the percentage of influence it has on forming your company image. The total of all the percentages should equal 100%.

Rate the following as image forming influences

Word of mouth	_____%		Employees	_____%
Brochures	_____%		Advertising	_____%
News stories	_____%		Appearances	_____%
The product/service	_____%		Sales staff	_____%

Your Image

Step 3: Identify your company image as your employees see it.

Answer from the perspective of your employees, or give a copy of this form to each employee and have each fill it out. It may be desirable to do this anonymously so no one will not feel obliged to give positive, but untrue, answers. Self flattery has no value in good marketing.

	Yes	Sometimes	No
This is a very enjoyable place to work.	( )	( )	( )
The owner really has the customer's best interests at heart.	( )	( )	( )
The owner really has the employee's best interests at heart.	( )	( )	( )
The products we offer are the very best we can provide.	( )	( )	( )
We really work to know as much as possible about what we sell.	( )	( )	( )
People would rather do business with us than our competition.	( )	( )	( )
The owners actively solicit suggestions and criticisms from us.	( )	( )	( )
We have never been deceptive or misrepresented our products.	( )	( )	( )
I never hear any negative comments about the owner.	( )	( )	( )

Step 4: Rate your company image.

Give yourself a 2 for each Yes answer, a 1 for each Sometimes answer, and 0 for each No answer in Steps 1 and 3. Total your scores for each Step and find its place on the table below. An *Average* or lower rating indicates you probably need to work on your image. As far as image is concerned, *Average* doesn't sell products. The questions which pulled your scores down are the places to begin.

	Excellent		Good		Average		Fair		Poor	
Customer Image Rating	26	23	22	21	20	19	18	17	16	15
Employee Image Rating	18	17	16	15	14	13	12	11	10	9

Advertising - The Action Plan

The advertising you create to accomplish your priorities should follow a logical progression. This progression is based on a few simple principles:

1. People will not buy something they don't like or care about.
2. People don't generally like or care about things they do not understand.
3. People can't be expected to understand anything they're not familiar with.

You shouldn't expect people to be motivated to purchase a product they are not familiar with by discounting its price.

The following chart represents the logical progression of advertising used at each stage of a product's life cycle. New products start at the bottom of the ladder because they need to build awareness. Older products, with established visibility, might start further up.

Based on its position on the advertising ladder, note which advertising tactics will aid your product in moving up the ladder. Although you can incorporate elements of all the tactics in your advertising, the main point should reflect its true position on the ladder. Don't try to move to the next level before you have effectively established yourself at the previous one. Plan your activities by quarter. It is important to allocate the majority of your advertising budget during the times when people normally buy the product. Planning activities by quarter also allows you to follow your natural progression up the ladder.

The image you *project* to your customers is half the battle in good marketing. The position you assume in relation to your competitors forms the basis of your image and is the heart of effective marketing.

Good marketers aren't content to duplicate other companies or be just another member of the pack. They seek their own unique niche in the customer's mind. Good positioning means building PREFERENCE for your products or services.

Advertising - The Action Plan

Step 1: Determine your competitive advantage.

Place a check beside those statements which you feel you or your products can legitimately claim, that is unique or superior to your competition. Concentrate on what makes you different from the competition and consider only those which benefit the customer. Check only those where you can answer yes:

_____ First	_____ Most attractive	_____ Most unique/unusual
_____ Largest	_____ Best service	_____ Most consistent
_____ Oldest	_____ The Best	_____ Most economical
_____ Friendliest	_____ Most convenient	_____ Best selection
_____ Highest quality	_____ Newest	_____ Most expertise
_____ Most reliable	_____ Only	_____ Best reputation
_____ Other _____		

Step 2: Position Reinforcements.

For each positive response listed in Step 1, identify things you can do to reinforce that market position:

A. _____

B. _____

C. _____

D. _____

E. _____

Step 3: Describe the market position you wish to achieve.

How do you want customers to see you in relation to your competitors? Is there anything you alone can claim to be that is unique or superior to your competitors?

_____

_____

_____

Step 4: List the steps you will take to reinforce this position.

A. _____

B. _____

C. _____

D. _____

E. _____

Using Media in Advertising

1. NEWSPAPERS

Advantages

- Tangible medium, reader can clip ad and save it
- Allows advertiser to include great detail
- Enjoys great credibility and acceptance

Disadvantages

- Circulation has steadily declined, doesn't equal readership
- Deadlines constrain copy and layout
- Passive medium. Reader can select what ads to read.

2. MAGAZINES

Advantages

- Can offer optimal target marketing
- Frequently highest quality production
- Allows advertiser to include great detail

Disadvantages

- Passive medium (see newspapers, above)
- Advertising clutter means low readership recall
- extreme deadlines constrain copy and layout

3. DIRECT MAIL/DIRECT ADVERTISING

Advantages

- Offers optimal target marketing
- Response rate can easily be measured
- Can cover every household

Disadvantages

- Traditionally low response rate
- Requires lengthy preparation and lead time
- Difficult to control delivery

4. YELLOW PAGES

Advantages

- Callers are already in market when they call
- Copy can be long, full of information
- High penetration (everybody has access to them)

Disadvantages

- Longest deadline lead time, inflexible
- Passive medium (see newspapers, above)
- Cannot include price information unless fixed over long period

5. SHOPPERS/PENNY SAVERS

Advantages

- Effective to reach buyers about to make decision
- Appeals to price conscious
- Allows advertiser to include a lot of detail

Disadvantages

- Small reach (limited readership usually duplicated in other print media)
- Frequently low quality production
- Rarely read thoroughly, discarded quickly

Using Media in Advertising

6. OUTDOOR/TRANSIT (Billboards)

Advantages

- Location
- Size, impact
- Highly effective for simple ideas

Disadvantages

- Inflexible, changes difficult
- Messages can physically deteriorate
- Both have negative image, subject to much regulation

7. RADIO

Advantages

- Reach, 95% of people listen in a week, 75% in a day
- Extremely good for targeting demographics
- Active medium (listener hears everything broadcast, can't opt not to hear commercials easily)

Disadvantages

- Advertiser cannot include much detail
- Proliferation of stations breaks up audiences/demos
- Certain day-parts of little value

8. TELEVISION

Advantages

- High production values available, creativity
- Highest reach per single exposure
- Can demonstrate product or service

Disadvantages

- Audiences increasingly fragmented (new channels)
- Increasingly limited to nighttime viewing
- Highest media costs

9. SPECIALTY ADVERTISING (caps, calendars, buttons, pens, etc.)

Advantages

- Ability to target into specific markets
- Usefulness of product insures longevity of message
- Allows for personalized messages

Disadvantages

- Limited space for messages
- Long production and delivery times
- Difficult to evaluate effectiveness

Advertising Media Advantages and Disadvantages

In any advertising campaign there are two elements: the medium (the path of communication) and the message (the idea being communicated). Good media use involves selecting the right medium to reach your audience. Newspaper is not always the best choice nor the only choice (although many small business owners tend to use newspaper exclusively). Using a mix of media can create a total advertising package greater than the sum of the individual parts.

Step 1: Copy and complete the following table.

Copy and complete for each medium you plan to use in your advertising.

Step 2: Prepare an advertising media evaluation.

Using the list of the advantages and disadvantages of various media located on pages 38 and 39, assess the media you plan to use in each of the following areas.

1. *Reaches current customers*
2. *Reaches new customers*
3. *Allows use of detail in an interesting way*
4. *High quality reproduction*
5. *Is an active medium*
6. *Has credibility with potential customers*
7. *A tangible medium - can be saved*
8. *Format allows flexibility in messages and visuals*
9. *Has instant impact and appeal*
10. *Allows the product to be demonstrated*
11. *Can target specific demographic groups*
12. *Has a reasonable production lead time*
13. *Can evaluate results*
14. *Not limited in terms of when you can use it*
15. *Messages can be remembered*
16. *Is cost-effective for your target market*

Step 3: Evaluate the relative strengths and weaknesses of each medium.

Note the major strengths and weaknesses of the media. Based on this table, rate each medium in overall terms and evaluate your current advertising, and determine if you are using the right media for your needs.

Step 4: Select the media you feel will accomplish your objectives.

Rate each of the mediums by its ability to accomplish your specific advertising objectives. You may only have one or two that rate highly. Your differing objectives may even require a mix of several media. Those that rate highly will become your primary media mix. Those that rate medium will become secondary media.

Advertising Media Advantages and Disadvantages

Step 1: Media being evaluated.

Medium:_____

Step 2: Relative effectiveness.

	Yes	Somewhat	No
1. Reaches current customers	( )	( )	( )
2. Reaches new customers	( )	( )	( )
3. Allows use of detail	( )	( )	( )
4. High quality reproduction	( )	( )	( )
5. Active medium	( )	( )	( )
6. Credibility with customers	( )	( )	( )
7. Tangible medium	( )	( )	( )
8. Format flexibility	( )	( )	( )
9. Impact and appeal	( )	( )	( )
10. Allows demonstration	( )	( )	( )
11. Targets demographic groups	( )	( )	( )
12. Reasonable production time	( )	( )	( )
13. Can evaluate results	( )	( )	( )
14. Not limited	( )	( )	( )
15. Memorable	( )	( )	( )
16. Cost-effective	( )	( )	( )

Step 3: Evaluating strengths and weaknesses.

Greatest strength of this medium _____

_____

Greatest weakness of this medium _____

_____

Overall evaluation of this medium _____

_____

Step 4: Media rating.

	High	Medium	Low
Ability to reach target audience	( )	( )	( )
Ability to present desired message	( )	( )	( )
Ability to accomplish objectives	( )	( )	( )
Overall rating	( )	( )	( )

Media Buying Fact Sheet

Advertising is any form of paid communication and promotion of your products or services. The purpose of advertising is to:

1. Attract Attention   *2. Present a message*   *3. Stimulate action*

Advertising is not always the best solution to all marketing situations. For example, you may live in a community which has no radio or television stations of its own. Buying commercials on a radio station in a nearby community, even if the signal reaches your audience, means you may be paying to reach a lot of people who will never buy your product. You may not want to advertise during certain seasons of the year because people don't buy then, or at certain times of the day because people aren't listening or watching.

When evaluating the use of advertising, ask yourself these questions:

1. Is there a particular period when most of the buying is done?
2. Is there a medium available that can zero in on your target market?
3. Can the product sell itself in the brief format most advertising employs?
4. Can you produce advertising materials of adequate quality and appeal?
5. Is the market receptive to advertising messages?
6. Do you have an adequate budget to spend on advertising?
7. Would advertising be socially or morally objectionable?

Advertising campaigns can consume large amounts of money in a very short time and accomplish nothing. Use a specific set of controls to govern when and where you will advertise. These controls should provide for a maximum allowable budget, an expected result in sales or goodwill, desired impact on visibility, duration of the campaign, anticipated effect on store traffic or inquiries, and allowable cost per customer reached. In the space provided at the right indicate your limits for each type of advertising you plan to do.

Most media representatives and advertising agencies rely on a basic fact sheet about their clients in order to effectively develop advertising messages and select media channels.

The following abbreviated work sheet provides a fast reference for the most important features of your company. It covers its advantages and other competitive information to be used when writing ad copy about the company.

Step 1: Identify the company.

Complete this work sheet if you plan to use advertising to promote your business.

Step 2: Evaluate the company's function and service.

Describe the physical and functional characteristics of the company. Include information on its intended purpose, basic form of operation, physical appearance, and quality of service.

Step 3: Competitive information about the company.

Answer the following questions about the company's primary competition. Include information about alternative companies that sell these products, characteristics that distinguish your company from its competition and your company's strongest selling points.

Step 4: Characteristics of the company's target market.

Who is the target market for the company. Describe by age, sex, income, occupation, education, and location. When do customers most often make purchases? Refer to page 14 for target markets.

Media Buying Fact Sheet

Step 1: Company identity.

Name of Company _____

Type of business _____ How long in existence?_____

Step 2: Company function/service.

What does your company do? _____

How well does it work? _____

How good does it look? _____

How good is the service? _____

Step 3: Competitive information.

List four competitive companies.

1._____   3._____
2._____   4._____

List the major products these competitors are selling.

1._____   3._____
2._____   4._____

Describe any recognizable or exclusive competitive advantages of your company.

_____

List at least four of your company's strongest selling points.

1._____   3._____
2._____   4._____

Step 4: Market characteristics.

Who are the TARGET customers for your company?

_____

When is the best time of year to promote the company?

_____

Your Advertising Theme

To be effective in your advertising you must develop an effective message to communicate to your customers. This message must explain who you are and why someone should buy your product in as simple a manner as possible. It must also stimulate the interest of the buyer.

People are bombarded with thousands of visual and audio messages every day. As a result they often "tune out" all but the most attractive or stimulating advertisements. Some simple concepts can help you get your message through to your customers.

Step 1: Use the following suggestions to outline your advertising themes.

a. *Plan around a single idea or thought* - Simple messages are best. Try to convey your message in a few well-chosen words.

b. *Identify yourself* - Mention your store or product name enough times in each ad to ensure it will be remembered.

c. *Be visual* - Pictures are not only interesting but help communicate the message better than words alone.

d. *Be consistent* - People can't relate to things that change each time they see them. They need to hear or see the same thing repeated several times before they remember it for any length of time.

e. *Speak to your customer's values and desires* - Find out what your customers *want*, and develop advertising that sells to these values.

f. *Be understandable* - Don't use too many words, or words that are difficult to understand.

g. *Sell the result, not the means* - People care *first* about what a product will do for them. Only afterward will they consider its particular features. To use an example cited by many marketing professionals, "People don't buy drills . . . they buy ways to make holes!"

h. *Put the reader in the ad* - Address the ad to the reader by using "you" in the copy. Instead of saying "This brewer makes great coffee," say "This brewer will make *you* a great cup of coffee!"

Advertising messages directed to commercial or industrial buyers need to address their three most common concerns.

1. *Risk* - Commercial/industrial buyers are very concerned about the effect their decision may have on their job and their status in the organization. Your advertising must assure the buyer that purchasing your product involves little risk.

2. *Conveniences* - Buyers for larger industrial firms make a multitude of decisions each day. The last thing they want is a complicated purchase procedure. In fact, buyers will continue with a more expensive provider for many years simply because they have a convenient procedure.

3. *Price* - Price is important to any purchaser, but it generally ranks third after risk and convenience. It is a rare buyer who chooses price without considering potential risks and the convenience of purchase/delivery first.

Your Advertising Theme

Step 1: Advertising Theme

a. What is your simple advertising message?

_____

_____

b. How should you identify yourself?

_____

_____

c. What is a good visual element of your product/business?

_____

_____

d. What should all your ads have in common?

_____

_____

e. Why do buyers need this product?

_____

_____

f. Can you summarize your message in ten words or less?

_____

_____

g. What is the positive result of using the product?

_____

_____

h. How can you put the reader in the ad?

_____

_____

Copythink

"Copy" is the term advertisers use to describe the body of text written for an ad. The copy will often clarify a headline or explain a picture, in addition to describing the product. Advertising copy should be interesting and should touch the buyer personally. Advertising copy should stress the reasons for buying your product or service. "Copythink" is designed to help you isolate the important elements for your ad copy, and provide an outline around which the actual advertising copy can be written.

Selling points are the physical attributes, or physical characteristics of a product that contribute to its desirability. Ideally, a product should have more than one selling point. Selling points include such features as size, shape, weight, packaging, color, texture, flavor, cost, variety, etc.

Benefits are the satisfactions derived from the product or service. Benefits include such features as convenience, availability, usefulness, appearance, prestige, familiarity, quality, speed or cost.

The following example illustrates the basic elements of Copythink.

>   *Example*: Pampers

>   *Selling points*: disposable, pre-packaged, plastic, have gathered or non-gathered legs.
>   *Benefits*: convenience, economy, easy, peace of mind, dry baby bottoms.

Step 1: Identify your product's selling points and benefits.

Refer to the product definition section beginning on page 16. Select the two most important physical characteristics of each product you sell and write them in the spaces marked "selling points." Do the same for physical benefits and write them in the spaces marked "benefits."

Scan the list and look for selling points or benefits common to all your products. Items which recur for more than half your products can be considered "organizational" or "business" selling points and benefits. Write the two most important from each column in the last set of spaces.

Copythink

Step 1: Selling points of your product

	Selling points	Benefits
Product name	_____	_____
	_____	_____
	_____	_____
Product name	_____	_____
	_____	_____
	_____	_____
Product name	_____	_____
	_____	_____
	_____	_____
Product name	_____	_____
	_____	_____
	_____	_____
Product name	_____	_____
	_____	_____
	_____	_____
Product name	_____	_____
	_____	_____
	_____	_____
Overall Business	_____	_____
	_____	_____
	_____	_____

Campaign Strategy Work Sheet

Good planning can save you time and money when you put your ad campaigns together. It will be a valuable tool when you are working with your selected advertising mediums.

Use the Strategy Work sheet to track your advertising and promotional efforts.

Step 1: Copy and complete this work sheet.

Use it in conjunction with the Media Buying Fact Sheet earlier in this workbook.

Step 2: Identify the product or service you will be advertising.

Step 3: Identify the customers you wish to target.

Step 4: Note the media you will use and when you will use it.

Step 5: Note the theme of the advertising.

Step 6: List the selling points and benefits if production is to be done.

Step 7: Note how the advertising should be illustrated.

Indicate what type of artwork you need, and the message you wish the advertising to convey. These should be consistent with your desired market position.

Step 8: Determine co-op availability.

Frequently, manufacturers offer to share the cost of any advertising which promotes their brand names. This is called "co-op" or cooperative advertising. Considerable documentation is required to obtain reimbursement, but most media representatives are well aware of the paperwork requirements. Note if co-op is available and if you have asked for and received documentation.

Note: You may want to develop these plans on a quarterly basis in order to accommodate changes in the buying season, or to coordinate several campaigns.

Campaign Strategy Work Sheet

Step 2: Product/service.

Product to be advertised:_____

Date_____ For time period_____ to_____

Step 3: Target.

Target market_____

Step 4: Media (attach separate sheets, schedules if appropriate).

Newspaper _____   Direct Mail_____

_____   _____

Radio _____   Outdoor _____

_____   _____

Television _____   Other _____

_____   _____

Step 5: Advertising message.

Copy theme_____

Step 6: Selling points/Benefits.

Selling points   Benefits

_____   _____

_____   _____

_____   _____

Step 7: How illustrated.

Describe art or visuals.

_____

_____

Describe desired message.

_____

_____

Step 8: Co-op advertising.

Co-op available?_____   Requested documents?_____   Received?_____

Public Relations - The Action Plan

Public relations is a planned effort to influence opinion through non-paid publicity. It is one of the most under-utilized tools for the small business owner. Public relations activities are valuable because they are relatively low-cost and enjoy a high level of credibility. Studies show that consumers more often believe what they read or hear in the news than they see or hear in paid advertising. Good public relations provides strong reinforcement to an existing customer base.

Step 1: Inventory your present public relations activities.

The following list represents some of the more common activities used to promote an organization through public relations. Describe those you have done in the past that worked, and list any ideas you might have for the future.

Events _____

_____

News releases _____

_____

Speeches _____

_____

Contests _____

_____

Audio visual presentations _____

_____

Literature/brochures _____

_____

Trade shows (indirect) _____

_____

Endorsements _____

_____

Public Relations - The Action Plan

Specialty items _____

_____

Sponsorships _____

_____

Annual reports _____

_____

Memberships _____

_____

Public Relations Opportunities

Many organizations maximize their use of public relations by keeping a calendar or check-list of potential opportunities for publicity.

The occasion need not be big to justify a call to the local newspaper or radio station. Many news directors are hungry for "offbeat" or "human interest" ideas.

Step 1. Plan for up-coming events and opportunities.

You may have the basis for a good news story already in place. Look for unusual things, different ways of doing business, unique products, etc. The following work sheet contains a list of common opportunities that could form the basis for a P.R. event or news release. Use this list to develop your own P.R. opportunities.

Step 2. Establish media contacts.

Make a list of the names of the news directors or chief reporters at each radio and television station in town. Find out who covers human interest or business stories for the local paper. Try to visit them at least quarterly and learn what they consider newsworthy.

When an opportunity does arise, prepare a news release and bring it with you when you visit your media contact.

Step 3. Establish service club/organization contacts.

Make a list of influential clubs and organizations in your area, and find out the names of their key representatives or directors. Call and arrange a time to meet with them to learn more about their organization. Determine if there are opportunities to make presentations about your industry or your business.

Public Relations Opportunities

Step 1: Event planning.

1. Company anniversary   When_____
   PR method recommended: ( )Event   ( )News Release   ( )Call to Media

2. New employee hired   When_____
   PR method recommended: ( )Event   ( )News Release   ( )Call to Media

3. Change of location   When_____
   PR method recommended: ( )Event   ( )News Release   ( )Call to Media

4. New product/service   When_____
   PR method recommended: ( )Event   ( )News Release   ( )Call to Media

5. Changes in operation   When_____
   PR method recommended: ( )Event   ( )News Release   ( )Call to Media

6. Employee promotion   When_____
   PR method recommended: ( )Event   ( )News Release   ( )Call to Media

7. Awards/Displays   When_____
   PR method recommended: ( )Event   ( )News Release   ( )Call to Media

8. Unusual circumstance   When_____
   PR method recommended: ( )Event   ( )News Release   ( )Call to Media

9. Other_____   When_____
   PR method recommended: ( )Event   ( )News Release   ( )Call to Media

Step 2: Media Contacts.

TV News Directors _____

Radio News Directors _____

Business Editor at newspaper _____

Step 3: Service Club/Organization Contacts.

	Contact		Contact
Rotary Club	_____	Kiwanis	_____
Lions	_____	Elks	_____
JCs	_____	Active 20/30	_____
Cham. of Com.	_____	Prof. Org.	_____
Bus. Club	_____	Other	_____

Public Relations Tools

The following three pages show samples of three common public relations tools. They include a public contact form, a news release format, and a public service announcement format. Read them thoroughly and begin to use them where applicable.

Public Contact

This can be a valuable resource in determining how your advertising is working, if your staff is performing effectively, and if your products are satisfying your customers. It is also a way to track questions and concerns. Adapt the form illustrated for use in your business.

News Release

Positive headlines can mean hundreds or thousands of dollars in increased sales. Most business people don't realize that many of the stories they see in the news about companies are simply the result of a phone call or news release.

News releases should be kept short. If the reporter wants more information, he or she will call. Put the information in a "who, what, when, where, why and how" format with the most important things first. If possible, use a quote or two. Sending a picture also helps. The following is a brief example:

> Joe Blow, Vice President of marketing for Premier Widgets, (*who*) won the coveted National Association of Widgeteers Marketing Excellence Award (*what*) last week (*when*) at the Association's national convention in Wagontire, Montana (*where*). Blow was presented the award by John Smith, Association President, as a result of his outstanding contribution to furthering widgets in the American workplace (*why*).

> Blow, who had been working with the Association for the past six months, remarked about the campaign " . . . (*a more detailed description of how*).

Ultimately, the newspaper editor will decide whether or not to do a story. Not every news release results in a story, but you must provide the information before you even have a chance at getting coverage.

Public Service Announcement (PSA)

Radio and television stations, although not required by the FCC, do devote a percentage of their air time to public affairs programming. PSAs are not advertising and you shouldn't try to use PSAs as a way to avoid buying radio or TV advertising. If you're trying to *sell* something with this approach, a sales representative is sure to call. But *do* make use of public service time to provide valuable information about services which you may offer free, or about activities your business is involved in that benefit the community. Remember this is intended to create visibility, not sell products. An example of an acceptable PSA subject might include the following:

> Premier Widgets, in conjunction with the Oregon Chapter of Worthwhile Causes, is sponsoring its fifth annual Rock Painting and Leaf Raking Festival this Saturday on the Downtown Mall. Events to be scheduled include . . .

> For more information on entering the Rock Painting and Leaf Raking Festival, contact Joe Blow at Premier Widgets, 555-1234.

Public Contact Report

Caller _____   Date

Address _____   Phone

Reason for call/visit: ( )Information   ( )Service   ( )Complaint

Received by_____

Summary of contact

_____

_____

_____

_____

_____

_____

_____

_____

_____

_____

_____

_____

_____

Action taken: ( ) Referred to   _____

              ( ) Resolved   How _____

              ( ) Incomplete   Why _____

              ( ) Pending   Next contact _____

Follow-up: ( ) No   ( ) Yes -   How _____

             Date of Follow-up _____

             Result _____

News Release Format

Today's date

Your name
Your title
Company name
Address
Your phone number

FOR IMMEDIATE RELEASE (or type here the date you want information released)

_____SAMPLE HEADLINE_____

(Double space - Use "who, what, when, where, & why format")

_____

_____

_____

_____

_____

_____

_____

_____

_____

_____

_____

END

(If your news release has two or more pages, type the word "MORE" at the bottom of each page until you reach the last page. Then use the "END." Use only one side of the paper for copy. Label and number each page.)

Public Service Announcement Format

(LETTERHEAD OR PLAIN WHITE PAPER)

Kill date (you do not wish announcement
used after this date)

Your name
Your title
Company name
Address
Your phone number

PUBLIC SERVICE ANNOUNCEMENT

(Double space - Describe event, activity or cause. Do not use more than two short paragraphs.)

_____

_____

_____

_____

_____

_____

_____

END

Personal Sales - The Action Plan

Advertising doesn't sell products, people do. Advertising helps make the job easier.

There is no substitute for personal service in good marketing. Advertising and public relations help to bring a potential customer to a point of feeling they want to buy a product or visit the store. The final act of making the sale depends on what happens *in* the store.

Customer service involves the attitude and actions of every employee, but most often focuses on the activities of your salespeople.

Step 1: Develop a comprehensive sales inventory.

The following tools will help you and your sales people become more effective in their sales efforts.

-   a. *Leads* - Leads, or prospects, are the lifeblood of any active sales effort. Leads come from three basic sources:
    1. Referrals from others.
    2. Advertising leads from a media placement.
    3. Coincidental leads resulting from a "cold call" or a chance meeting.
-   b. *Service* - 90% of good salesmanship is related to servicing the account. A recent study showed that 68% of all lost sales were attributable to a lack of service or a poor attitude on the part of employees. Price, on the other hand, accounted for less than 15%.
-   c. *Organization* - You won't be successful in developing leads if you aren't organized.
-   d. *Communication* - You must communicate regularly with your sales people to keep them informed of product or policy changes and improvements.
-   e. *Attitude* - The image you project is a direct reflection of the attitudes held by your sales people. Try to instill a positive, helpful attitude in your sales staff.
-   f. *Appearances* - It's important to project a good image if you want people to believe you're good.
-   g. *Knowledge* - It's important to be knowledgeable about all aspects of your product. Many sales are lost because the salesperson simply says "I don't know." Of course, no one can know everything, so if a salesperson is forced to say "I don't know" they should immediately follow up with "but I'll find out." That shows you care.
-   h. *Support* - Don't just throw salespeople out on the street and expect them to perform. You must provide organizational, financial and material support. Support materials are discussed more fully on pages 67 and 69.

Complete the inventory on the following page regarding your own sales program.

Step 2: Describe the overall objectives for your sales program.

It is important that salespeople understand clearly what they are working toward. Sit down with your sale-speople and review your organization's marketing mission on page 7 and your sales forecasts from page 79. It would be wise to use their assistance in preparing these two work sheets anyway. They are the ones who have to promote your vision to the customer and they should feel involved in its development.

Personal Sales - The Action Plan

Step 1: Sales inventory.

1. What is your current process for generating leads?

_____

_____

2. How do you evaluate service?

_____

_____

3. How do you organize your sales effort?

_____

_____

4. How do you communicate with your sales staff?

_____

_____

5. How do you monitor staff attitude?

_____

_____

6. How would you change staff appearance?

_____

_____

7. Does your sales staff have good product knowledge? Do you provide continuing training?

_____

_____

8. How do you plan to support your staff organizationally, financially and materially?

_____

_____

Step 2: Overall sales objectives.

_____

_____

_____

_____

Sales Materials

Printed materials are not a substitute for good salesmanship, but printed materials must often represent you to your prospective customer. The quality of your printed materials should equal the quality of your personal sales staff.

Step 1: Identify the printed sales materials you currently use.

Include any materials you do not produce directly, but may receive from a supplier or manufacturer. Note if you have the option of having the name of your company added or imprinted on them.

Step 2: Note how you use your sales materials.

Planning can keep you from wasting sales and help keep your costs down. Include:

- *When to use them*

- *Under what circumstances*

- *Who is to receive them*

Step 3: Identify the printed sales materials you need.

After you have evaluated what you already have available, you may decide you need additional sales materials. Confer with your sales staff to determine if additional sales materials are necessary, and if so, have them assist you in developing them.

Assign the preparation of each piece to someone on the sales staff and note the date when you propose to have them complete the work. Have them find out if one of your suppliers or distributors has sales materials they can make available to you.

Be sure to include sales materials in your marketing budget. This is an area often overlooked during the crush to prepare advertising campaigns.

Sales Materials

Item	Step 1 **Currently use**	Step 2 **How used**	Step 3 **Need**
PRICE LISTS	( )	_____ _____ _____	( )
CATALOGS	( )	_____ _____ _____	( )
BROCHURES	( )	_____ _____ _____	( )
BUSINESS CARDS	( )	_____ _____ _____	( )
STATIONERY	( )	_____ _____ _____	( )
MAILERS	( )	_____ _____ _____	( )
ANNUAL REPORTS	( )	_____ _____ _____	( )

Passive Sales

Passive selling represents your final attempt to persuade the customer to buy at the point of purchase. Passive selling is distinct from active selling in that it does not require a sales representative. Sales clerks are included in the list only because too many clerks don't look for opportunities to sell the product—they merely bag the goods and take the money.

Step 1: Identify the passive sales materials you currently use.

Step 2: Note how you use your sales materials.

Package design - Is often the only chance a product has to catch the eye of a passing customer. When trying to decide between two or three competitive products, the most attractive is chosen most often.

Point of purchase display - An "in-store advertising campaign" designed to assist in attracting attention, and provide additional incentive for impulse buying.

Hand-outs - Similar to direct mail in function.

Posters/banners - Great attention grabbers, both in the store, and outside where they can be seen from the street.

Window display - The first objective of a promotional campaign is to get people into the store. The better the window display, the better the store traffic.

Sales clerks - Clerks can be "order takers" or "order makers." Don't just ring up the sale. Ask if the customer needs anything else. Make suggestions, try to cross-sell. But *always* be polite and friendly. This will turn a passive salesperson into an active sales person.

Step 3: Identify those materials you need.

Determine how you plan to use each piece, and when.

Passive Sales

Item	Step 1 Currently use	Step 2 How used	Step 3 Need
PACKAGE DESIGN	( )	_____ _____ _____	( )
POP DISPLAY	( )	_____ _____ _____	( )
HAND-OUTS	( )	_____ _____ _____	( )
POSTERS/BANNERS	( )	_____ _____ _____	( )
WINDOW DISPLAYS	( )	_____ _____ _____	( )
SALES CLERKS	( )	_____ _____ _____	( )

Promotional Incentives

Incentives are those things a marketer does to increase the likelihood of making a sale now, versus some point in the future. Incentives can be considered to be "dependent" promotional options because they don't really work effectively by themselves. Incentives work best when used *with* another form of promotion.

Incentives can often breath new life into products at the declining end of their life-cycle. However, the misuse, or uncoordinated use of incentives can be wasteful, and have a negative long-term impact on further marketing activity.

Step 1: Identify the promotional incentives you currently use.

Step 2: Note how you use your promotional incentives.

Samples - Free samples build the habit of customers using your product and make them feel good about your product at the same time.

Sales (price) - Sale prices imply that the buyer can TEMPORARILY acquire a higher value product at less cost. Don't offer products at sale prices all the time.

Coupons - Coupons represent a great price incentive and work best when they have a time limit incentive.

Time limits - Time limits are one of the most powerful incentives you can use. Nothing gets people to act faster than knowing they only have a short time to make a decision.

Package elements - Coupons on packages, or special two-for-one packages can be very attractive incentives.

Display elements - See Point-of-Purchase on page 68.

Gifts - Free gifts can be effective incentives. But use gifts where they are appropriate. Giving away a toaster with a checking account is no longer as effective as it once was, but a free toy in a box of cereal will always keep kids buying.

Games and contests - People always love to play games. Using games and contests can help motivate people to purchase your product.

Step 3: Identify additional incentives you can use.

Determine how you plan to use each incentive, and when.

Promotional Incentives

Incentive	Step 1 Currently use	Step 2 How used	Step 3 Can use
SAMPLES	( )	_____ _____ _____	( )
SALES PROMOTIONS	( )	_____ _____ _____	( )
COUPONS	( )	_____ _____ _____	( )
TIME LIMITS	( )	_____ _____ _____	( )
PACKAGE ELEMENTS	( )	_____ _____ _____	( )
DISPLAY ELEMENTS	( )	_____ _____ _____	( )
GIFTS	( )	_____ _____ _____	( )
GAMES & CONTESTS	( )	_____ _____ _____	( )

Your Pricing

The price you charge for a product is governed by controllable and uncontrollable factors. In its simplest form, pricing strategy involves figuring out how much it costs you to buy or make the product, add your cost of doing business, then add your margin for profit.

In order to effectively price your products/services you must first have a detailed outline of the costs for making, buying, or selling your products. Cost-based pricing is probably the system most often used by those entering business for the first time.

Cost-Based Pricing Forms

1. Cost-plus pricing - The TOTAL cost you must incur to buy the product, plus an allocation for those costs you incur every month whether you sell anything or not, plus an additional amount for profit.

   EXAMPLE - $12.95 net cost + $3.31 overhead + $1 net profit = $17.26 retail price

2. Mark-up pricing - The cost you must incur to buy the product is "marked-up" by adding on an additional percentage for gross profit.

   EXAMPLE - $12.95 net cost x 1.333 (25%) gross profit = $17.26 retail price

Although both cost-plus and mark-up pricing have their advantages, neither one really takes the consumer into account when setting the price.

Prices based strictly on the production and operating costs of the business often fail to take advantage of the enormous profit potential inherent in consumer demand.

The following pages will help you develop information about the financial operation of your business. Use your records, or have your accountant help you. Try to work in averages wherever possible. You may need to divide a yearly total by 12 to come up with a monthly average. If you are starting a business, you will have to project your expenses.

Fixed expenses (also known as Overhead) are monies you must pay out regardless of whether you perform any services or sell any products. Examples of fixed expenses include rent, utilities, loans, etc. Variable expenses are those costs which are likely to change depending on the amount of business you do. Examples of variable expenses might include the cost of raw materials, production costs, distribution costs or commissions. Salaries have also traditionally been considered variable expenses because many companies add or lay off employees in response to their sales volume. However, most small businesses keep a few employees on all the time, so you will probably want to consider salaries as a fixed expense.

Some other pricing terms you will encounter include:

Net Cost - This is the amount of money it costs you to make or acquire the product. It does not include anything for Overhead and thus can be a deceptively low figure.

Gross Cost - The Net Cost plus a portion of the Overhead. A much more reasonable figure to use since it allows for the fact you need to pay for things like the rent.

Retail Price - This is the final price the consumer is charged for a product. It includes all production costs, variable costs, margins, and mark-ups for the manufacturer, the wholesaler and the retailer.

Gross Profit - The difference between the Net Cost and the Retail Price. For some companies with low production costs and high fixed costs, the Gross Profit can be impressively large.

Net Profit - This is the difference between the Gross Cost and the Retail Price. This is the final "no strings attached" profit for the company. High Overhead expenses can eat up the Gross Profit and leave only a small Net.

Margin - Another way of talking about Profits.

Determining Fixed Expenses

Step 1: Determine your monthly fixed expenses.

In the table on the next page, write in the appropriate spaces the amount you spend each month on the fixed expenses. Since these expenses are fixed, they should not change from month to month. If you do not currently have an item as a fixed expense, leave the space blank.

Step 2: Determine your total monthly overhead.

"Overhead" is the figure you must pay out each month to cover fixed expenses. It is simply the sum of all the items listed in Step 1.

Step 3: Figure your total yearly overhead.

Multiply the monthly overhead by 12 to arrive at the amount you must pay just to keep your business open for one year. This figure does not include any expenses for actually making or distributing anything.

A Note About Demand-Based Pricing

Pricing by cost alone, although assuring that you will recover your expenses, does not take into account the enormous profit potential resulting from demand.

Demand-based pricing is based on the number of products you expect to sell under a specific set of circumstances. These can include promotion, packaging, fads, special interest, or some competitive factor. Unfortunately, demand-based pricing is a tricky practice for even the most experienced professionals since demand can change on a moment's notice. As you gain more experience in the market you may want to consider adding some "demand-based factor" into your price. It is generally advisable to use cost-based pricing as the backbone of your overall strategy.

Determining Fixed Expenses

Step 1: Fixed expenses.

Office Operation

Rent	$_____	per month
Utilities	$_____	per month
Phone	$_____	per month
Supplies	$_____	per month
Insurance	$_____	per month
Accounting	$_____	per month
Legal	$_____	per month

Payroll	$_____	per month
Marketing	$_____	per month
Leases	$_____	per month
Maintenance	$_____	per month
Corporate Taxes	$_____	per month
Furniture & Fixtures	$_____	per month
Loans % Notes	$_____	per month
Bad debts	$_____	per month
Other Expenses	$_____	per month

Step 2: Monthly overhead.

TOTAL MONTHLY OVERHEAD $_____ per month

Step 3: Yearly overhead.

TOTAL YEARLY OVERHEAD (monthly x 12) $_____ per year

Determining Fixed Expenses

Step 4: Allocate a portion of your fixed expenses to each product, or product line.

If a product represents 25% of your annual income, then allocate 25% of your fixed cost to it. This method does not take into account the labor-intensive costs associated with some products, but it will work as a starting point.

The best way to calculate the percent of a number is to multiply that number by the percent you want to find, expressed as a decimal. For example, 15% of 50 would be:

$$50 \times .15 = 7.5$$

Allocating fixed costs by product line

TOTAL YEARLY OVERHEAD $_____ (from the previous page)

    Fixed costs associated with product #1 $_____ per year

    Fixed costs associated with product #2 $_____ per year

    Fixed costs associated with product #3 $_____ per year

    Fixed costs associated with product #4 $_____ per year

    Fixed costs associated with product #5 $_____ per year

    Fixed costs associated with product #6 $_____ per year

    Fixed costs associated with product #7 $_____ per year

    Fixed costs associated with product #8 $_____ per year

    Fixed costs associated with product #9 $_____ per year

    Fixed costs associated with product #10 $_____ per year

Determining Variable Costs

Step 5: Copy this page and complete for each product you sell.

PRODUCT _____

Step 6: Insert the total number of units sold last year.

_____ Units/Individual services (Use estimates if necessary)

Step 7: Figure variable costs for the last year.

If you do not have figures for the past year, make your best estimate of the costs you probably would have incurred.

A. If You Are a Retailer:

Total wholesale cost to you	$_____
Total cost of delivery of products to you	$_____
Total inventory or storage costs	$_____
Total shipping or delivery to customers	$_____
Other costs incurred during the sale of product	$_____
TOTAL YEARLY VARIABLE COSTS	$_____

B. If You Are a Manufacturer:

Total cost of raw materials	$_____
Total cost of delivery of materials to you	$_____
Total cost of manufacturing the product	$_____
Total cost of packaging	$_____
Total inventory or storage costs	$_____
Total shipping or delivery to wholesaler/retailer	$_____
Other costs incurred during the manufacture of product	$_____
TOTAL YEARLY VARIABLE COSTS	$_____

C. If You Deal in a Service:

Total cost of materials used	$_____
Total cost of job related labor†	$_____
Total transportation/delivery to customers	$_____
Other costs incurred while providing service	$_____
TOTAL YEARLY VARIABLE COSTS	$_____

† Do not include the salary of anyone who is paid regardless of the workload.

Step 8: Calculate the per unit variable costs.

Total Yearly Variable Costs		# of Units/Services Sold		Per Unit Cost
$_____	÷	_____	=	$_____

Cost-Plus Pricing

Step 9: Figuring a cost-plus price.

The cost-plus price is essentially the *cost* of making or providing a product (variable expenses) plus a portion of the *overhead* (based on that product's percent of the total operation), plus a portion of the *profit* you wish to make. In cost-plus pricing the overhead, the variable expense, and the profit are not dependent on each other. Any one can be changed without affecting the other two.

For Product _____

a. Expected sales of units   _____ units per yearb

b. Total yearly fixed expense $_____
    (from page 66)

c. Per unit fixed expense (b÷a) $_____

d. Per unit variable cost (from page 68) $_____

e. Unit Net Cost (c+d) $_____

f. Expected annual profit $_____

g. Profit per unit (f÷a) $_____

    UNIT RETAIL PRICE (e+g) $_____

Step 10: Figuring a marked-up price.

In mark-up pricing you take the actual *cost* of making or providing a product, and multiply it by one or more percent *factors* which represent overhead and/or profit. In this way, the amount you add for overhead or profit is proportional to the cost of the product. In other words, expensive products receive a proportionately larger share of the overhead and profit automatically. The amount added is also related directly to the cost of the product. You cannot change the cost without also affecting the amount of overhead and profit. This method is useful for pricing one of a kind items, or services which are not consistent enough in price to allow cost-plus pricing.

For Product _____

a. Expected sales of units   _____ units per year

b. Total yearly fixed expense $_____
    (from page 66)

c. Per unit fixed expense (b÷a) $_____

d. Per unit variable cost (from page 68) $_____

e. Unit Net Cost (c+d) $_____

f. Gross Profit Margin (d÷e) x 100   _____%

    UNIT RETAIL PRICE (e x Profit Mark-up Factor) $_____

PROFIT MARK-UP FACTORS

5% = 1.053	15% = 1.176	25% = 1.333	33% = 1.493
10% = 1.111	20% = 1.25	30% = 1.429	35% = 1.538

Forecasting Sales

Forecasting sales is critical to your business from both a management and sales point of view. If you don't know how much you plan to sell in the next 12 months, you can't plan how much to spend. Remember to be realistic in your projections. Look for trends by reviewing your own records or industry figures.

Step 1: Sales History.

Copy and complete this table for every product you sell. List the total number of units sold during each of the previous five years. If you are just starting up, try to get some industry information on average company sales or consult with someone who is likely to know what product sales have been. Take particular note of any trends in yearly sales, such as overall declines or increases.

Step 2: Assess Current Demand.

Examine monthly sales figures for the last twelve months. Starting with the first two months, figure the percent increase or decline in sales. If the first month's sales are smaller than the second month's, simply divide the first month by the second month. The resulting decimal represents the percent INCREASE in sales. If the second month is smaller, the equation requires an additional step. Divide the second month by the first month, *then* take the resulting decimal and subtract 1 to get the percent DECREASE in sales. *(Remember, always divide the smaller month by the larger month.)* The following example with January earnings of $10,000, February earnings of $20,000, and March earnings of $15,000 will illustrate the two equations.

If SECOND month is larger	January's $10,000 ÷ February's $20,000 = .5 or a 50% INCREASE in sales. **(Write in as +50%)**
If FIRST month is larger	March's $15,000 ÷ February's $20,000 = .75 .75 - 1 = -.25 or a 25% DECREASE in sales. **(Write in as –25%)**

Add up all the monthly percentages. If a percent is negative, subtract it instead of adding it to the total. In a bad year it's possible to wind up with a final total that is negative. Divide the total by 12 to arrive at a yearly trend.

Step 3: Projected Year's Sales.

Using the trend information derived from Steps 3 and 4, project the number of units you expect to sell in the next 12 months. If you feel confident your marketing efforts will result in an increase in sales, increase this figure by that degree of confidence. Divide the total units by 4 to arrive at an average number of units you expect to sell each quarter.

Step 4: Make Seasonal Adjustments.

Starting with the average quarterly figure, adjust each quarter's units up or down to match the trends you calculated in Step 4. As you add to one quarter, you must subtract from other quarters to keep the total unit figure the same.

Step 5: Calculate Quarterly Income.

Insert the adjusted quarterly figures in the appropriate places. Multiply the quarterly figure by the per unit retail price to arrive at the quarterly income figure.

Step 6: Calculate Total Year's Income.

Add together the four quarterly incomes to arrive at the total projected yearly income.

Forecasting Sales

Step 1: Sales History.

PRODUCT _____

	4 Years Ago	3 Years Ago	2 Years Ago	1 Year Ago	Last Year
Total Units Sold	_____	_____	_____	_____	_____

Step 2: Current Demand.

Jan _____%   Feb _____%   Mar _____%   Apr _____%   May _____%   Jun _____%

Jul _____%   Aug _____%   Sep _____%   Oct _____%   Nov _____%   Dec _____%

Yearly Trend _____%

Step 3: Projected Sales This Year.

Total Units to Sell   _____ + 12 = _____   Average Units Per Month

Step 4: Seasonal Adjustment.

First Quarter	Second Quarter	Third Quarter	Fourth Quarter
_____	_____	_____	_____

Step 5: Quarterly Income Projected.

First Quarter Units	_____	x Unit Price =	$_____	First Quarter Income
Second Quarter Units	_____	x Unit Price =	$_____	Second Quarter Income
Third Quarter Units	_____	x Unit Price =	$_____	Third Quarter Income
Fourth Quarter Units	_____	x Unit Price =	$_____	Fourth Quarter Income

Step 6: Year's Income.

$_____ **Total Year's Income**

Budgeting

Even a modest promotional effort requires some expenditure of resources. The two most valuable resources you have to invest are money and time. What you lack in one resource you can often compensate for with the other. In other words, if you don't have a lot of money to spend on advertising, you can devote additional time in public relations or sales. Business owners who don't have much time, generally compensate with money. But in either case, how much you "spend," and where you "spend" it, should be carefully planned to help get the biggest "bang for the buck!"

There are several ways to determine how much to "spend" on marketing:

Percentage of sales - This can be an average figure for your industry, such as 6%, which you determine based on past performance or by using industry sources.

Activity or task - In this method, the tasks which you need to accomplish determine the budget. Each task is priced out and the total becomes the marketing budget.

Competitive parity - This is the "paranoia" theory of budgeting. You determine what the competition is spending and spend a similar amount.

Arbitrary spending - You spend on impulse without any plan or justification.

Default budgeting - You spend what is "left over" on marketing.

None of these methods is ideal. However if you use a blend of the top three, you can create a budgeting "checks and balances" system that works pretty well.

Step 1: Develop a percentage-based marketing budget.

Transfer your projected total income for the next year from page 71. Multiply this figure by the percentage you wish to devote to marketing (new businesses will probably require a higher percent than established ones). Also, be sure to change the percent to a decimal before you do the multiplication. For example, 25% = .25 when used in a calculation.

Step 2: Develop a task-based marketing budget.

Add together the amounts you need to spend each quarter to accomplish these tasks. You can get estimated costs for planning, printing, media, artwork, and production from each of your suppliers. Make your totals as accurate as possible.

Step 3: Develop a competitive-based marketing budget.

You can't estimate how much your competitors are spending unless you know what they are doing. Collect samples of their advertising and get estimates from your suppliers on the cost to produce similar pieces.

Step 4: Formulate a comprehensive marketing budget.

Compare the three different budgets you have calculated (using an average as a reference point). If there is a wide discrepancy between one or all of these amounts, use your judgement to determine which way you should adjust to reach a final comprehensive budget.

Budgeting

Step 1: Percentage-based budget.

    a. Projected income from page 71 $_____

    b. Percent to be allocated for marketing   _____%

    Percentage-based marketing budget (a x .b) $_____

Step 2: Task-based budget.

    Cost of tasks planned in first quarter $_____

    Cost of tasks planned in second quarter $_____

    Cost of tasks planned in third quarter $_____

    Cost of tasks planned in fourth quarter $_____

    Total of tasks planned for the year $_____

Step 3: Develop a competitive-based marketing budget.

Amount spent by your major competitor in:

Radio	$_____	Direct mail	$_____
TV	$_____	Stationary	$_____
Newspaper	$_____	Packaging	$_____
Magazines	$_____	Displays	$_____
Billboards	$_____	Brochures	$_____
Catalogs	$_____	Other	$_____

Total spent by competitor in a year $_____

Step 4: Formulate a comprehensive monetary marketing budget.

    a. Percentage-based budget $_____

    b. Task-based budget $_____

    c. Competitive-based budget $_____

    Average budget amount (a+b+c÷3) $_____

Final Comprehensive Budget (adjusted average budget) $_____

Amount of budget to be allocated to:

First Quarter	Second Quarter	Third Quarter	Fourth Quarter
$_____	$_____	$_____	$_____

Budgeting

Step 5. Prepare quarterly promotional budget allocations.

Using the information you have just prepared, allocate your budget over the four quarters. You may wish to refer to the information on page 35 for a list of tasks and activities you must accomplish.

Regarding the allocation of time in your marketing budget

As already noted, time is one of the two main resources you have for marketing. Since no one can tell you how much time you should spend on marketing, or how much time you have, you must allocate this resource according to your own priorities. The following tips, however, might help you in allocating your marketing "time budget."

- The higher up you are in the organization, the more time you should try and devote to "personal marketing," that is, getting out and meeting people. People are usually more interested in meeting the head of an organization than a staff member.

- Service businesses, particularly professional and business services, benefit greatly from participation in chambers of commerce, business, and civic organizations. However, you must be an active member in order to get the benefit. Active participation gets you noticed and respected; passive membership just eats up time.

- Service businesses rarely have a "product" they can show when selling. This means they wind up selling themselves. One of the best ways to sell yourself is to become established as an expert. Some good ways to do this include teaching a class or holding a workshop on your subject. You might also volunteer your services to a civic organization as a way of gaining visibility in your specific job area. You would be surprised how fast word gets around.

- Try to get out of the office at least once a day. It may be lunch with the chamber of commerce, an early morning reception, or an afternoon meeting with a civic group. Don't view these things as wastes of time. They are valuable opportunities to be seen; and in marketing, being seen is one-third of the goal.

- Entertainment can be a great form of marketing, particularly for salespeople. The secret is not to run up a huge expense account while doing it. Be creative in your choice of business entertainment and you can save money. A lot of products and services are sold on the golf course, over a few drinks, or after a quiet dinner at home.

- Spend some time marketing *inside* the organization. The time you invest in getting to know your employees and their needs is an investment in good image. Employees take their attitudes with them as they serve customers.

- Take the time do do your planning. An hour spent in good planning can save several hours of "fixing" time when something goes wrong. An hour of planning can also save hundreds of dollars in poorly executed advertising. Planning *is* as important as everyone says it is.

Budgeting

Step 5: Quarterly budget allocations.

First quarter budget from Step 4, page 73. $_____
   Amount allocated to:

Radio	$_____	Direct mail	$ _____
TV	$_____	Stationary	$ _____
Newspaper	$_____	Packaging	$ _____
Magazines	$_____	Displays	$ _____
Billboards	$_____	Brochures	$ _____
Catalogs	$_____	Other	$ _____

Second quarter budget from Step 4, page 73. $_____
   Amount allocated to:

Radio	$_____	Direct mail	$ _____
TV	$_____	Stationary	$ _____
Newspaper	$_____	Packaging	$ _____
Magazines	$_____	Displays	$ _____
Billboards	$_____	Brochures	$ _____
Catalogs	$_____	Other	$ _____

Third quarter budget from Step 4, page 73. $_____
   Amount allocated to:

Radio	$_____	Direct mail	$ _____
TV	$_____	Stationary	$ _____
Newspaper	$_____	Packaging	$ _____
Magazines	$_____	Displays	$ _____
Billboards	$_____	Brochures	$ _____
Catalogs	$_____	Other	$ _____

Fourth quarter budget from Step 4, page 73. $_____
   Amount allocated to:

Radio	$_____	Direct mail	$ _____
TV	$_____	Stationary	$ _____
Newspaper	$_____	Packaging	$ _____
Magazines	$_____	Displays	$ _____
Billboards	$_____	Brochures	$ _____
Catalogs	$_____	Other	$ _____

Working with Consultants

Marketing or advertising consultants are outside advisors who are experts in their respective fields. They give their advice and are paid for this service. They have the advantage of being independent and impartial.

An advertising agency is essentially a consultant with the facilities to perform some or all the tasks required to perform their job. For example, a marketing consultant may counsel you on a course of action but take no active role in its implementation. An advertising agency, on the other hand, can assume the responsibility for performing whatever actions are recommended.

Consultants usually charge by the hour or the project. Hourly fees can range anywhere from $50 or $75 an hour, all the way up to $200 or $1,000 a day plus expenses. Per-project fees usually include an agreed upon set of tasks, and a time limit to complete them. You should arrange to have all overruns and additional expenses approved BEFORE they are completed. Hourly fees are usually used when the advice is intermittent, conducted over short periods, or does not require the extensive use of materials. Per-project pricing is usually more cost effective when large amounts of time or materials are to be used.

Step 1: Copy the Agency Evaluation Form.

Complete this form for each advertising agency you interview. At the very least you should interview two agencies, and ideally three or four. Ask friends or business associates for recommendations about advertising agencies. Check the ads in the newspaper or on the radio. Determine which ads you like and find who produced them.

Step 2: Evaluate the agency by the criteria listed.

It is rare to find just the right agency to work with the first time you look. This work sheet gives you a basis on which to evaluate different agencies.

Working with Consultants

Step 1: Agency.

Agency_____

Address_____

Phone_____

Name/s of principle/s_____

Step 2: Evaluation.

EVALUATION CRITERIA	COMMENTS
( ) List of current clients	_____
( ) Samples of work done	_____
( ) References from clients	_____
( ) References from media	_____
( ) Agency brochure	_____

In the spaces provided make notes for future reference.

Has this agency has done advertising for a similar business?

_____

Can I work with the individuals who would be handling my account?

_____

What experience does this agency have which is applicable to my business?

_____

What suggests that these individuals have an understanding of my needs?

_____

How does this agency handle billing? What is their track record in paying bills?

_____

How creative is this agency's work?

_____

Timetable

Use this work sheet to determine the progression of your promotional efforts. Stick to the time lines you set and you will ensure that the jobs get done. This will also help you determine if you have too many activities and not enough time or staff to get all the jobs done.

Step 1: Identify key activities.

Make a list of your key objectives in advertising, public relations, and sales management. These could be campaigns you want to launch, events you want to hold, product changes you wish to implement, or customer research you need to undertake.

Step 2: Assign responsibility for each activity.

For each activity you have defined, assign supervision of its implementation and completion to one person within the company.

Step 3: Set a scheduled starting date.

Decide when you will begin work on each activity. Note whether or not other activities will be performed at the same time.

Step 4: Set a scheduled finish date.

Decide when you plan to have the activity completed. For on-going activities such as advertising, you can set a date on which your intensive involvement will end.

Step 5: Evaluate the effectiveness of your efforts.

After completion of the activity or campaign, determine if it accomplished the goal. The goal might be financial, or related to image building and visibility. In any case, it is an important element of your marketing program to constantly measure its success and establish new goals for the future.

Timetable

Step 1 Activity	Step 2 Person	Step 3 Start	Step 4 Finish	Step 5 Evaluation

Some Resources to Use in Your Marketing Planning

This section includes a list of some common sources of information you can use to conduct your marketing.

Advertising Planning Calendar

Frequently a local newspaper publishes an advertising planning calendar. This calendar will list by month all pay periods, holidays, and most frequently purchased goods and services. Since sales promotions benefit from coinciding with paydays, this can be a valuable resource for tracking and projecting, not just print, but all media advertising plans.

Media Packets

Most media salespeople carry packets of information regarding their particular station's rates, markets, etc. If you wade past all the sales pitches, you can often find a lot of very useful information regarding the market for a particular station.

Magazines and newspapers also provide media packets, but you often must write to receive them. It is well worth the stamp to request a media packet from a national magazine. These publications spend thousands of dollars each year gathering data for their advertisers.

SRDS (Standard Rate and Data Service)

The SRDS is a "catalog" of national media services. In it you will find a listing for every magazine (or newspaper, radio station, etc. depending on the volume you use) in the country. You will also find information regarding editorial content, advertising rates, mechanical requirements for advertising, the names of who to contact for information, and circulation figures. It is an invaluable resource for evaluating media. You can generally find one in the reference section of any public or university library.

The Small Business Administration (SBA)

This federal program specializes in providing both financial and advisory assistance to small businesses throughout the country. You can get in touch with the SBA through your local community college or write:

> U.S. Small Business Administration
> 1441 L Street N.W.
> Washington, DC 20005

Associations

Most industries have national associations. If you already belong to an association, write and ask them to send information about the market for your product or service. Many national associations spend thousands of dollars every year gathering data for their members. Use your association!

The Small Business Development Center (SBDC)

Your local Community College or University probably has a Small Business Development Center specifically established to provide services and resources to the small business community.

If you cannot locate an SBDC in your area, you can contact the national Association of Small Business Development Centers at:

> Association of Small Business Development Centers
> 1050 17th Street N.W.
> Suite 810
> Washington, DC 20036

Some Resources to Use in Your Marketing Planning

SCORE (Service Corps of Retired Executives)

SCORE is a national organization of retired business people who volunteer their time to advise small business owners.

SCORE volunteers often have many years' experience in operating both large and small businesses. They can often provide practical insights few others possess. They really understand the problems of running a business.

Internal information

Many business owners fail to take advantage of information resources which already exist within their own companies. Business records, client lists, and past employees are all important resources for developing information about your business and its market.

Additional Resources

The following books may be useful in providing additional information on marketing.

Competitive Strategies and *Competitive Advantage*, two books by Michael Porter, Free Press
Consumer Behavior: Implications for Marketing Strategy, Hawkins, Best, and Coney, Business Publications
Do It Yourself Marketing Research, Breen and Blankenship, McGraw-Hill
Effective Public Relations, Cutlip, Center, and Broom, Prentice-Hall
Guerrilla Marketing, Levinson, Houghton-Mifflin
Handbook of Innovative Marketing Techniques, Seltz, Addison-Wesley
How to Advertise, Kenneth Roman and Jane Maas, St. Martins Press
Insiders Guide to Demographic Know How, American Demographic Press
Marketing for Non-profit Organizations, Kotler, Prentice-Hall
Marketing Government and Social Services, Crompton and Lamb, John Wiley & Sons
Successful Marketing for Small Business, Cohen and Reddick, AMACOM
The Marketing Problem Solver, Chase and Barasch, Chilton Books

Order Form

Other workbooks prepared by the Oregon Small Business Development Center Network to assist small business owners and potential owners include:

Your Business Plan - Written for the small business owner or manager who has never prepared a working business plan. This workbook helps clarify the goals, objectives, and strategies necessary to run a successful small business. Business principals and practices are discussed, and step-by-step instructions guide the small business manager in the preparation of an actual business plan.

Your International Business Plan provides a method that small business owners can use to expand their business into international markets. This workbook helps managers evaluate the potential for success in other markets. It serves as a tool to help prepare an organized plan to reach untapped markets.

Su Plan de Negocio - Hispanic small business owners are among the fastest growing segment of our economy. *Su Plan de Negocio* is the Spanish version of *Your Business Plan*, and was translated to help Hispanic entrepreneurs develop their small business and ensure greater success and profitability.

Books may be ordered from: Oregon Small Business Development Center Network
99 West 10th Avenue
Eugene, OR 97401-3017   Phone: (503) 726-2250

ORDER FORM

TITLE	QTY	PRICE	TOTAL
Your Business Plan	_____	$20.00	$_____
Your Marketing Plan	_____	$20.00	$_____
Su Plan de Negocio	_____	$20.00	$_____
Your International Business Plan	_____	$20.00	$_____
Please add $1.50 <u>per book</u> for postage & handling			$_____
TOTAL	_____		$_____

NAME: _____

ORGANIZATION: _____

ADDRESS: _____

CITY/STATE/ZIP: _____

P.O. # _____ PHONE: _____

(Make check payable to: OSBDCN/LCC)